TO THE
HEART
OF THE
MATTER

TO THE
HEART
OF THE
MATTER

The 40-Day Companion
to Live a Culture of Life

Shawn D. Carney

Cappella
Books
Nashville, Tennessee

For information write to Cappella Books,
P.O. Box 50358, Nashville, TN 37205.

ISBN 978-1-7327417-4-4

Cover design: Jam Graphic Design
Author photos: Andrea Fisher
Editor: Noelle Mering
Interior layout, typesetting, and e-book: LParnell Book Services

Manufactured in the United States of America

20 21 22 23 24 • 10 9 8 7 6 5 4 3 2 1

DEDICATION

*For my children, words cannot express
the joy and motivation you give your mother and me
to live a culture of life . . . every day.*

Contents

~ ~ ~

Foreword

"Love is . . . the fundamental
and innate vocation (call) of every human being."
— Pope John Paul II

~ ~ ~

In March of 2004, I joined my Sisters to kneel at the front of Saint Patrick's Cathedral in New York City, professing our vows to protect and enhance the sacredness of human life as a fully-recognized Catholic religious community of women.* In July of that same year, sixteen hundred miles away in College Station, Texas, a group of fervent pro-lifers bowed their heads around an old wooden table for an hour of prayer. For each of us, in those singular moments, a grace that had been percolating for some time was confirmed by the Holy Spirit— a new grace for the cause of life.

---

* The Sisters of Life were founded on June 1, 1991; after years of living and "testing" the grace of our foundation, on March 25, 2004, we were confirmed by the Church in the authenticity of the charism of life that we had received.

We both found and were confirmed in the reality that being pro-life today can no longer be just an activist activity. It's been tried—and the result, generally speaking? Burnout, bitterness, and disappointment. In a world battered and bruised by the forces of darkness—darkness greater than our human strength—a spiritual response is needed.

To the Heart of the Matter may be the first-ever public work that articulates what this spiritual response is, what it is to be pro-life in daily living. It's a response that is fresh and integrated and strikingly bold in its simplicity. It's a way that is new and yet as old as the Christian life.

What is this way, exactly? It's a way of love. It's learning the primacy of being over doing. It's rediscovering the power of love in the little things: caring for our families, daily sacrifices, prayer and intercession, celebration, mercy, forgiveness, and speaking the truth in love. It's letting the joy of Life—Life who is a person, Jesus Christ—permeate our lives. It's leaning our full weight on the One who conquered the grave, throwing self-reliance to the wind. It's living as if everything matters . . . because it does. For, indeed, because of the Incarnation, nothing again would be casual or small. Jesus has filled everything with light, He is the final word, and history belongs to Him.

In Mark 9, Jesus tells His disciples, "This demon can only be cast out by prayer and fasting." What Shawn Carney helped to begin in 2004 as a movement of prayer, fasting, community outreach, and vigil in response to a spirit of contempt for human life has blossomed into a far-reaching communion of souls. As one who has lived the pro-life cause from the inside out, Shawn knows where its power lies: in the little things. Whatever we do with love and prayer—no matter our state in life—can build and is building a culture of life. We matter. Our prayer matters. And what we do with our love matters.

You'll find that this book shines a light on that which is most essential in the fight for life: that being pro-life today means first witnessing to what it is to be fully, joyfully, unabashedly human . . . for, as Saint Irenaeus said, "the glory of God is man fully alive."

This book is a call to hope. It's a call to living with intention. It's a call to love.

God raises up people in every age to meet the needs of the day. The time for activism alone has passed; now is the time for saints. Now is the time for men and women who have been transformed by Love. So let us not be afraid. Let us lift up our chins. Let us live like we've never lived before.

Mother Agnes Mary Donovan, SV
Superior General, Sisters of Life

I grew up with six brothers.
That's how I learned to dance—
waiting for the bathroom.
— Bob Hope

Introduction

First Things First

~ ~ ~

In a memorable scene, Forrest Gump simply and confidently tells his embittered and despairing former lieutenant, "I'm going to Heaven, Lieutenant Dan." Unimpressed, Lieutenant Dan replies with a smirk, "Oh? Well, before you go, why don't you get your butt down to the corner and get us another bottle of Ripple?"* Obediently, Forrest departs saying, "Yes sir."

As we strive to live for Heaven with simplicity and focus, we are often reminded that the world prefers a bottle of Ripple. This is an old struggle; however, the degree to which the world has grown hostile to what we ought to hold most dear is unprecedented. This hostile environment makes *your* daily activities, routine, and priorities more important than ever before.

What is it that has created such an opportunity for your daily heroism?

The assault on the family.

---

* wine

1

The current assault is unlike any in history. We see it in the opposition to the natural and divine understanding of marriage, gender, children, sex, and sacrifice. This assault is philosophical, institutional, and even bloody. Out of 195 countries, abortion is legal in all but 5. With the support and funding of most of those governments, 56 million people are killed *every* year. It is unprecedented by the sheer numbers alone.

But it is unprecedented in another way as well. Unlike prior wars, genocides, or mass executions that have darkened human history, this holocaust is directed at the most unexpected and helpless of victims: our own children.

It is not hyperbolic to say that abortion is not only the defining moral issue of our time, but it is the defining moral issue of *all* of time. Of course, there are many injustices and brutal assaults on the dignity of the human person; I am not claiming my genocide can beat up your genocide. But I am saying that the violence of the act, the helplessness of the victim, the corruption of the fundamental relationship of parent and child, the global support of the powerful, and the scale of lives claimed—56 million every year—put us in dramatically unchartered waters.

Despite this grim reality, I am not a nut who runs around my dry cleaner or grocery store yelling at innocent bystanders about the injustice of abortion. Nor am I a "the world is going to Hell in a handbasket" kind of Christian. I am genuinely joyful, hopeful, and inspired by all that is going on in the pro-life movement. But I am not naive, and neither are most people I encounter in this great work.

We didn't get here overnight, and it won't be fixed overnight. We might ask ourselves, who are we to fix it anyway? We have jobs, kids, grandkids, lawns that need cutting, milk that needs purchasing, and our endless and ever-growing to-do lists. We are busy. And, frankly, 56 million abortions every year is overwhelming.

After all, I barely make enough time for daily prayer, oil changes, or reading this book. What can I possibly do?

The answer lies with only six words that give us daily spiritual guidance in the noisy and difficult times in which we live. They were spoken by someone who did not get overwhelmed by the circumstances she faced but kept first things first and entrusted all to Jesus Christ.

> *Do small things with great love.*
> – Mother Teresa

Ironically, Mother Teresa was sometimes accused of not doing enough for the poorest of the poor.

No one grows up wanting an abortion, and no one grows up wanting to work in the abortion industry. I've been outside more than 450 abortion facilities as a result of 40 Days for Life—forty days of prayer, fasting, and peaceful vigil outside of abortion facilities—spreading to over 850 cities in sixty-one countries. We have seen 1 million volunteers around the world help close more than 100 abortion facilities, save nearly seventeen thousand lives, and help two hundred abortion workers have a change of heart and leave their jobs.

I have seen women and men go in for an abortion from every walk of life, and the common theme is simple: *pain*. Pain fuels the abortion industry, and most often that pain started at home. We simply cannot have abuse, divorce, loss of faith, promiscuity, and the destruction of marriage without casualties.

Abortion is the symptom of the destruction of the family, and family is restored with love.

Many people complain to me that they are unable to do enough to help end abortion. They want to do more and sometimes feel guilty for not doing more. The truth is that if we don't put first things first in our daily lives, it will not matter what we do. If our lives, jobs, duties, and routines are not done with great love, we are not really pro-life because we are not really living an interior life. We are only activists trying to make it through the day alone, not realizing God is with us, for us, and in us.

I encounter saints and heroes every week who are ending abortion not by speaking or writing about the culture of life but by *living* the culture of life every day by doing small things with great love. Most of them don't realize it, but by being faithful to their commitment to Christ daily in prayer, work, and family—by doing small things with great love—they attack the culture of death. They go to the heart of the matter.

I am often asked, "What can I do with the little time that I have to help end abortion?" This book is a simple daily guide of small actions and prayer intentions to help focus our efforts. It is broken up into forty days, a chapter for each day. They are designed to be used any time of year or can serve as a daily companion for Lent or a 40 Days for Life campaign. They are simple and to the point—or, I should say, to the heart of the matter. They are small ways, accessible to each of us, to help end abortion, restore the family, and change the world for the greater glory of God.

These are difficult times but not hopeless times. We are here in this time in history for a reason.

Let's get started . . .

Day 1

Don't Be a Wimp

~ ~ ~

"Don't be a wuss."

"Quit complaining."

"Suck it up."

"Get over it."

These phrases conjure up stereotypes of a certain unsympathetic militancy. Our instinct might be to respond with an eye roll or the protest, "You don't understand."

I am thirty-seven years old, and most of these sorts of sentiments are supposed to be offensive to my generation. However, it seems in our noncommittal, excuse-making culture that we likely do not hear these statements often enough. Our inner pendulum tends to swing so far toward the sensitivity end of the spectrum that we are unable to be called out, changed, or told to just get it done. In short, we've lost the virtue of fortitude.

The pro-life movement is unique in that it demands a sense of relentless urgency. Every thirty seconds a baby is lost to abortion. But abortion has also been going on for five decades and seems, to some, to be here to stay. This can tempt us to feel paralyzed, but we do not have that luxury. We need fortitude.

Whether we have small kids, no kids, grown kids, kids who love us, kids who despise us, jobs we like, or bosses we want to shove off a cliff, we must commit to defend life on some level—and see to it that we live out that commitment. Much is at stake!

There are not lines of people out the door to go pray at an abortion facility, participate in a march, or volunteer at a local pregnancy center. Unlike more popular issues, such as feeding the poor and supporting cancer research or the Special Olympics, working for the pro-life movement is polarizing. Abortion is different, which means when you commit to doing something to fight it, then you are different. Being different requires fortitude and an ability to overcome the many excuses that insert themselves into our heads.

Let's start by committing to do something for the unborn, then let's follow through with it. With the many other things that are asked of us, we often don't say no enough. But we must say yes to this. Our future, our children, our families depend on our giving a meaningful and determined yes to defend those who have no voice but ours.

~ ~ ~

Daily Scripture:

Be on your guard, stand firm in the faith, be courageous, be strong.
— *1 Corinthians 16:13 NABRE*

Daily Intention:

Let me be firm in my commitment to pray every day for an end to the injustice of abortion.

Spilled Milk

~ ~ ~

I have eight kids.

From the time we dated, Marilisa and I wanted a lot of kids, and we have been greatly blessed. We also have no recollection of someone not needing something.

Throughout my travels people always comment (with varying levels of appropriateness) on the number of kids I have. From the predictable, "Do you know what causes that?" to the old, "Did you intend to have that many?" I have heard it all.

Our life is not chaotic or out of control. Our kids were not all delivered on our doorstep by Saint Peter in the middle of the night. With that said, we have had several phases in which we juggled three kids, three years old and under. Occasionally we've joked about driving ourselves to the local psychiatric clinic and being committed (particularly after long hours in the van).

Though our homelife is busy, constant, and often loud, it is happy and peaceful. However, there is one thing that drives me nuts that I will complain about to you: spilled milk.

I hate the sight of spilled milk, I hate cleaning spilled milk, and I hate the avoidability of spilled milk. While it tends to be the worst during the stage when a kid moves from a sippy cup to a "big kid" cup, it is not contained to that stage. I have threatened to make a nine-year-old use a sippy cup.

We all speak out against the big injustices of racism, violence, or abortion. But what are the small, normal battles in each of our days? What is your spilled milk? Doing what is tedious or inconvenient out of love for our families and for God is how we change the culture from the ground up. It is also what affirms our littleness in God's plan. This is the irony of motherhood being so belittled today. Mothers do the daily work that will have the greatest impact on the future of the world, and yet our culture often wonders why they don't get a real job.

The state of the family is a mess, and God has given us many ways during the day to clean up the mess, literally. Let us not belittle, underestimate, or avoid these small things.

~ ~ ~

Daily Scripture:

"For as the heavens are higher than the earth,
So are My ways higher than your ways
And My thoughts than your thoughts."
– *Isaiah 55:9*

Daily Intention:

Let me use my small pains today as a reminder to pray for all children scheduled to be aborted this day.

No Making Sense of It

~ ~ ~

Do you remember when you were (hopefully) sick to your stomach seeing the Empire State Building lit up in pink? It was not for breast cancer awareness or any other worthy cause but rather to celebrate New York's deeper departure from reality with the state-legalized killing of a baby at forty weeks.

This was followed by Gov. Ralph Northam in Virginia describing—in casual and downright creepy detail—how infanticide takes place when a baby survives an abortion. From there, America saw state after state in a race to the bottom to be the most "progressive" and pro-abortion state in the country.

I sat at my desk stunned, staring at the screen when I read the initial report. This new wave of further normalizing abortion and infanticide was literally unbelievable. Watching Northam, who is a pediatrician (I don't recommend him for your kids), calmly talking about abandoning a baby on the table to die was disgusting. Watching Gov. Andrew Cuomo in New York smile, laugh, and celebrate the most barbaric act of violence against the most defenseless human beings served as a gut check.

People tried to explain why these experts and politicians who dress so well and sound so nice were calmly speaking about declining medical help to a baby girl who survives an abortion. Or why they were justifying a "need" to abort a fully formed baby as a woman dilated at thirty-nine or forty weeks.

My advice to anyone attempting to explain their point of view was simple: "STOP."

As we live our daily lives, raise our kids, take care of our parents, or apply to college, we do so to enhance life, to improve life. When we mow the lawn or attend a nephew's eighth birthday party at a jungle gym and try a new ice cream, we are enhancing life. Can Cuomo go into a jungle gym with his nephew the day after signing this bill? Can he eat ice cream with his kids or grandkids? I don't know, but what I do know is that to slaughter a baby or refuse medical attention to a newborn who is minutes old is cruel and barbaric. It cannot be explained away and is undeserving of any attempt to do so.

We are seeing what a culture of death is capable of. It turns us into monsters. Do not give the coldhearted the credibility of treating barbarism as worthy of anything other than condemnation. Call it for what it is: evil. Point people to reality. Ask them if they have ever seen an ultrasound or held a newborn.

Do not tolerate their intolerance of children. We must speak up, plainly and lovingly, in our homes, offices, soccer games, or wherever we encounter any defense of these atrocities.

Panic is at the top and at the bottom of the abortion industry. We don't panic. We pray, fast, trust God, speak, and act.

The devil is never satisfied, not even with abortion. He does not just want the baby to die; he also wants to see people justify it and rejoice in it. We must pray, fast, show up, and love our families. That is the most reasonable response to a panicking culture that is taking its anger out on women and unborn children.

~ ~ ~

Daily Scripture:

"Indeed, the light of the wicked goes out,
And the flame of his fire gives no light."
   – Job 18:5

Daily Intention:

I will not underestimate the evil depths we are capable of when we dehumanize children. I will be their voice today and speak up for them when the situation demands it. Let me never underestimate the power of living my life through my simple duties of loving my family and neighbor.

Day 4

I Want to Go Home

~ ~ ~

Every person in the world has an identity.

It is not liberal or conservative or vegan or gay or open minded or traditional or any of the many groups in our label-drunk society. We are all, whether we acknowledge it or not, one thing: *pilgrims*.

We are not meant for permanence in this world, and that reality is waiting for us. On Ash Wednesday we have the most uplifting Scripture for any cynical Irishman: "For you are dust, and to dust you shall return" (Genesis 3:19).

We are pilgrims looking for one thing: home.

There is no home in the parking lots of abortion facilities. Women walk from their cars through facility doors, fearful and despairing. Men either never show up or drive them there but then abandon them shortly after paying (this occurs often and the woman calls a cab).

There is no home with those who support abortion. Choice, reproductive rights, autonomy, my body, a decision between a woman and her doctor—all these reasons given by the abortion industry shout one consistent message to women: you are alone. This is on you, about you, and something only you will live with. You are as alone as you will ever be, and that often is most felt in the recovery room.

There is no home in the relationships that lead to abortion. At times, tragic circumstances involve rape and abuse, but most abortions involve men taking advantage of women without respect for their bodies and souls and women in search of attention and affection. These are not relationships of love but of use.

Every corner of the abortion industry is homeless, but we are pilgrims in search of home. We long to be respected, comforted, and loved. Our journey ends at home, the home we were made for: Heaven. That is the heart's deepest longing, and the foreshadowing of that Home is how we find home in this life.

Whether you are married or single, have kids, grandkids, or no kids, our home is a vessel that prepares us and those around us for Heaven. Jesus Christ came to us through a home. There is nothing more important we can do than create a home that prepares us for our eternal Home. That is the best pro-life commitment we can make. Not having it has sent many in our culture in search of home in all the wrong places.

~ ~ ~

Daily Scripture:

"In My Father's house are many dwelling places; if it were not so, I would have told you; for I go to prepare a place for you. If I go and prepare a place for you, I will come again and receive you to Myself, that where I am, there you may be also."

– John 14:2–3

Daily Intention:

Today I will go home, call home, or text home to tell someone how much I love them.

Day 5

Boys Will Be Boys

~ ~ ~

You've heard the above cute phrase when referring to little boys finding new ways to play army, build a Lego structure, or surprise tackle you for no reason. Such boyish innocence is a fun and beautiful part of boys growing up to be men.

Today there is a deficiency of men. Many grew up without fathers in the home. Some were never taught such essential things as how to view women respectfully or change a tire. The danger of boys without fathers is that sometimes they never grow up—they become adult boys.

And our culture has plenty of examples. Adult boys are disrespectful, lazy, irresponsible, undisciplined, and view women as sex objects. And few things enable adult boys more than the seemingly consequence-free sex the abortion industry promises.

I once heard a priest speaking to a group of college men say that sexual temptation for men goes away ten minutes after death. To remain chaste is a struggle to greater or lesser degree for most men their entire lives.

It is easy to avoid the struggle and give in to the opportunities to lust, which are accessible to pretty much everyone these days. But chalking up this behavior to "boys will be boys" ignores the deep and varied wounds that are the inevitable consequences of this deceptively easy path.

There is another aspect to abortion that many men don't anticipate. Some have shared it with me. The reality is, when a guy decides he is going to engage in premarital sex with multiple women, he risks not only both of their dignity and self-respect; he risks being the father of an aborted child.

Men have no rights when it comes to abortion. I've shared this with men who tearfully begged me to get their girlfriends or wives out of the abortion facility. I wrote about some of these powerful encounters in the book *40 Days for Life*. In other cases, women have had an abortion and never told the fathers they were even pregnant. I've heard repentant men talk about the sleepless nights they have now because they suspect a former sexual encounter might have ended at an abortion clinic.

The world does not emasculate men; we do it to ourselves by the standard we set for ourselves. Men do not have to bend or cower to the whims of the world that tell them sex is casual and people may be used as objects. Real men humble themselves before God and do what is right. They pray for and with their girlfriends, wives, sisters, mothers, children, and grandchildren. They defend the weak with courage and strength. They

19

put others first and themselves last. We men know the peace that comes when we do this and the pain when we don't.

Abortion is not a woman's issue only. Nine men on the Supreme Court forced legalized abortion on America. Most abortion doctors are men, and many women feel they have no other option than to have an abortion because of the absence of a man or the presence of an adult boy who says nothing but the lame, "I'll support you in whatever you decide" (while he quietly hopes she will abort the child to make things easier on him).

We men are called to the exact opposite of such adult boys; we are called to lead and to sacrifice self in the process. Jesus Christ is our example. Saint Paul tells us, "Husbands, love your wives, even as Christ loved the church and handed himself over for her to sanctify her, cleansing her by the bath of water with the word" (Ephesians 5:25–26 NABRE).

If we are called to marriage, our greatest honor is to love our wives. When we do that, we will be able to defend them, our children, and our communities against the onslaught of attacks against the family. No one can be a man for us; it is our decision to make today and every day in this struggle to serve, lead, and love as Christ did.

~ ~ ~

Daily Scripture:

When I was a child, I used to speak like a child, think like a child, reason like a child; when I became a man, I did away with childish things.

— *1 Corinthians 13:11*

Daily Intention:

I will encourage a young man, either by thanking him for the good he is doing or teaching him by example or word how to be a better man.

Day 6

Fear of What?

~ ~ ~

There are three good reasons for *not* going out to peacefully pray at an abortion facility. Here they are:

1. You physically cannot go out. You are home-bound, sick, or lack transportation to get there.

2. You have anger issues and a criminal record. (Please stay home!)

3. You do not have the emotional capacity to go due to a past abortion experience.

These are good reasons, but today we focus on the folks *not* on this list. Most likely that is you and me.

Your reason was my reason. It was also every 40 Days for Life volunteer's reason for initially hesitating: *fear*.

Fear can paralyze us and prevent us from giving a courageous witness to God's love. If you haven't gone out to pray, it is most likely due to fear. This is not a guilt trip; it's an acknowledgment that you are normal. I can list off many things that are better to do with a Saturday (the days when most abortions take place because of the abortion doctor's schedule). There's college football, grocery shopping, lawn work, or smoking pork spareribs all day in your backyard. While all of these should be done and are pro-life in the right context, showing up to the abortion facility still matters. Gravely.

Our presence makes a tangible, life-saving difference. Former Planned Parenthood employees, including Abby Johnson (who was a Planned Parenthood director and an Employee of the Year before having a conversion and walking next door into my office), said that the no-show rate for an abortion appointment (typically 20 percent) goes as high as 75 percent when people are out there praying. This compelling fact was even included in the major motion picture about her story, *Unplanned*.

Who needs fear? A 75 percent no-show rate! How many babies are alive today because someone showed up to be a witness to the beautiful reality that women do *not* have to have an abortion? Let this be a great light to guide us from our fear out onto the sidewalks. The busier we are, the harder it is for us to get there, the more God will use that time.

~ ~ ~

Daily Scripture:

I command you: be strong and steadfast! Do not fear nor be dismayed, for the LORD, your God, is with you wherever you go.

— *Joshua 1:9 NABRE*

Daily Intention:

I will commit to pray at an abortion facility in the next month for thirty minutes.

Fear of God

~ ~ ~

Our comforts and endless desires to get what we want have transformed our perception of God from an all-powerful, all-knowing, all-loving God, who is both just and merciful, into a nice guy who would never get in the way of our desires.

When God is merely nice, we have no reason to fear Him. But the Scriptures tell us repeatedly that fear of the Lord is the first step to wisdom (see Psalm 111:10).

God is the creator, and we are the creature. When we reverse these roles, we head down a road that is bottomless, a road that we blindly construct as we go. Destruction snowballs when we crown our desires as king; we move from promiscuity to deviancy, abortion to the trafficking of baby body parts.

Your fear of the Lord in a world that has no fear of the Lord goes a long way. It is truly countercultural.

God is more than nice; He is the Father who keeps His promises, small and large alike. He loves us and our families more than we can imagine. He is to be feared because He is full of glory and power. He is Life itself.

Just as we cannot look directly at the sun burning, we can only imagine what His burning love looks like. To say that we fear the Lord is not to say that God is an angry old man who hates homosexuals and abortionists. Nor are we rubbing our hands together waiting to rejoice when He sends His lightning bolts to kill evildoers. It is an acknowledgment of the reality that God is God and we are not, and that this reality should prompt us to trust Him even at the expense of our own comforts and attachments. It is a reality that can be difficult to remember in a world with too much technology and not enough of a moral compass.

Fear of the Lord requires humility and helps us not to be blind to the humanity and helplessness of a baby, born or unborn. In seeing and reverencing who God is, we see ourselves and one another as we truly are: loved, irreplaceable, and made in His image.

~ ~ ~

Daily Scripture:

And to man He said, "Behold, the fear of the Lord,
    that is wisdom;
And to depart from evil is understanding."
    – Job 28:28

Daily Intention:

Today I pray for fear of the Lord. He is the Author of Life. Without Him I will never end abortion or have hope in a culture that has forgotten His power and awe. In the fight for life, let me fear only sin.

Day 8

In Solidarity

~ ~ ~

In our modern preoccupation with health, wellness, feeling good, looking good, low carb, low sugar, low fat, organic, vegan, vegetarian, it can be surprisingly refreshing to remember that inevitably we will die.

Of course, eating well and exercising are good things, which can improve and prolong our lives, but like most good things, they can become an obsession and, prolong as we might, our journey will come to an end. While it might make sense to keep our love for ice cream and bacon in check for now, it is comforting that barbecue is sure to be at the heavenly feast, enjoyed guilt free.

The martyr Thomas More said it best right before he was beheaded: "A man may very well lose his head and yet come to no harm—yea, I say to unspeakable good and everlasting happiness."

Because of what awaits us, we need not fear harm now. Our lives here are a gift, and we can use this gift to stand in solidarity with those who have been deprived of it.

In my book *The Beginning of the End of Abortion*, I lay out abortion procedures in detail based on the testimonials of abortion doctors. You would not wish it on your greatest enemy. It is violent, bloody, and horrifying with respect to both the act itself and the innocence of its victim.

With 56 million abortions per year, it can be easy for the numbers to overwhelm and paralyze us. We generally do not see these victims. It is a hidden holocaust. And who can relate to 56 million of anything? But we can pick one baby to spiritually adopt, give her a name, and carry her daily in our thoughts and prayers.

This helps foster a deep gratitude for our own lives. We will one day join these children in death, and long after we are gone, few will remember we ever lived. We have but one true home in Heaven. Rather than being morbid, our daily reflection on the reality of death is a signpost pointing us to the reality that we are not made for this world and every day is a gift. Let us use this gift of our lives to remember those who have lost theirs and work with our prayer and witness so that others might be spared.

~ ~ ~

Daily Scripture:

For here we do not have a lasting city, but we are seeking the city which is to come.

– *Hebrews 13:14*

Daily Intention:

I will spiritually adopt a baby scheduled to be aborted today, name him or her, and remember that today my life is a gift to be cherished until I find rest in my eternal Home.

You Aborted Beethoven!

~ ~ ~

They can be good at getting kids' attention, but I really don't like those gotcha stories.

You know the ones I'm talking about. The speaker acts as if he's telling a story about a normal couple with abnormal circumstances. The couple is poor, sick, running from communists, avoiding being abducted by aliens . . . whatever it is, they are barely making it when the woman gets pregnant. The drama and suspense increase (as listeners sit on the edge of their seats).

The saga continues with the revelation that the baby has a diagnosis or future imprisonment or fascists coming to their door or endless other problems no human could possibly bear. Then comes the set-up question: "Given the circumstances, should this woman have an abortion?"

The intensity is high when someone from the audience says, "Well, I can understand the difficult—" Abruptly, the speaker cuts off the audience member and blurts out, "Congratulations! You just aborted Beethoven." I have heard it done with so many celebrities or historical figures (the most famous example really is Beethoven).

These stories are sensational, albeit interesting, but I don't care for them much. I always feel bad for the struggling woman in the crowd who chose life but whose kid is a loser. Or the woman whose kid is seriously disabled and can barely communicate, much less write a book, compose music, become president, or land on the moon.

Abortion is tragic enough without it happening to the extremely talented or famous. I understand the interest in such stories, and they can be effective at turning on the light for some folks. Still, our lives are not valuable because we could be Beethoven; our lives are valuable because each of us is a gift from God. Whether your kid is top of his class or dumb as a brick, he or she is loved, cherished, and unrepeatable. They don't need to be Beethoven; they need to be who God made them to be.

Parents who choose life at the last moment are often embarrassed they ever considered abortion and grateful to God that He rescued them from that dark place. They do not have the expectation that little Teresa will turn out well because she is so lucky to be here. Our careers, grades, or basketball skills do not determine our value. At some point we have all looked down on people and wondered what they contribute to society. But what we can contribute is not the true measure of our worth, and our devaluing them speaks more to our weakness than to theirs.

~ ~ ~

Daily Scripture:

The base things of the world and the despised God has chosen, the things that are not, so that He may nullify the things that are.

— *1 Corinthians 1:28*

Daily Intention:

Today I resolve to be grateful for those who are marginalized, disabled, or viewed as having little worth. They may not be Beethoven, but they are still miracles.

All Grown Up

~ ~ ~

Aside from those who are doing abortions, most people want to save a baby from abortion.

That's why we have seen more than 1 million people participate in 40 Days for Life. I have had the honor and joy of holding more than a dozen babies saved during a 40 Days for Life campaign. I've seen pictures of hundreds and heard stories of thousands who have been saved at the last moment.

At stake in every abortion is the life or death of a baby. So, I thought.

A few years ago, I finished a speech for a post-abortion recovery ministry. Between the long travel day, the speech, and the numerous conversations that followed, I found myself exhausted and heading for the door at the end of the evening. A woman stopped me as I was leaving and expressed her gratitude to God for all 40 Days for Life had done, and her amazement that the campaign started in College Station, Texas, in 2004 and was now approaching one thousand cities.

"And I got to be part of that first campaign in 2004," she stated emphatically.

"You did?" I replied studying her face to see if I could place her. "What year were you at Texas A&M?"

She said, "No, I didn't go to A&M, and I didn't go out to the vigil during that first 40 Days for Life. I went into the Planned Parenthood to have an abortion. I went in, saw all of you outside and just couldn't do it. I left knowing that you all had no idea that you saved my baby boy. But I also knew that the opportunity would come one day to let you know. So, can I introduce you to my son?"

I was speechless and no longer cared how tired I was as she brought her teenage son over to meet me. There is nothing like holding a baby saved from abortion or even just seeing a picture of a baby who was saved. In speeches prior to this moment, I made the point that we are saving not just babies but future college students, future parents, grandparents, teachers, football coaches, and on and on. At this moment, though, I realized those had been only words; I had just been making a point. Now, that point was standing in the flesh talking to me about the sports he played and which colleges he was planning to apply to.

We talked for a while, and as I started to leave, I told the mom, "Hey, if you ever come down to College Station—"

She cut me off with an abrupt tone and said, "No, I will never go back; it brings back too much pain of how close I got to that abortion. I was in a dark place and could never go back. I can't even look at a Planned Parenthood, especially that one."

I smiled and realized she didn't know. "No, I wouldn't take you to the vigil to pray; in fact, we don't have a campaign there anymore. That Planned Parenthood where you almost had an abortion closed in 2013."

"Are you serious?" Tears were filling her eyes.

"Yes, and you should know that the building now serves as the headquarters of 40 Days for Life."

She broke down crying and through her sobbing said slowly, "That is the perfect use for that building. God is so good."

I was reminded of the small but profound point that in so many ways we must be patient when it comes to abortion. When she got my attention that evening, I was not excited to talk to her. I was being selfish.

It was not a good ending to the evening because I got to hear this great story—we're not entitled to results or to great stories. It was a good ending because she needed to speak, she wanted to introduce her son, and she was able to learn that this place that had haunted her memory had been redeemed. In the process I got shamed for being selfish and was reminded that our timelines, be they for an evening or for a lifetime, are not ours to dictate.

~ ~ ~

Daily Scripture:

God said, "This is the sign of the covenant which I am making between Me and you and every living creature that is with you, for all successive generations."

— *Genesis 9:12*

Daily Intention:

Let me never forget that abortion doesn't kill only a baby but an entire future. When I am selfish or inconvenienced today, let me remember that any given moment of my life does not belong to me.

Day 11

Keep Your Rosaries Off My Ovaries

~ ~ ~

Standing up for life is hard. Standing up for abortion is harder.

Those who support abortion pin themselves in a corner against science, reason, Scripture, and natural law. Supporting it is quite difficult. I've been screamed at from short distances and civilly disagreed with in emails, but the content is always the same: avoidance of the issue at hand.

Abortion advocates cannot talk about their product. It's amazing what you hear, and do not hear, when you just listen. They adamantly push for the very thing they refuse to discuss. Abortion must be allowed, but the actual procedure is taboo to talk about. Instead they insult you, what you stand for (or what they think you stand for), and your religion.

The Rosary (a traditional Catholic prayer that meditates on the major events in the life of Christ) cannot escape their wrath. The first time I heard "Keep your

38

rosaries off my ovaries" I burst into laughter. I had heard many things said in anger, but as I listened to what they were chanting I was surprised by the absurdity of it. A fellow pro-lifer at the vigil that day remarked that it was not funny. I agreed, though I couldn't help but be encouraged that they had abandoned healthcare, women's rights, privacy, and bodily autonomy for rosaries and ovaries.

That is a good sign for the cause of life. Prayer exposes them; it looks behind the curtain at an abortion industry rooted in madness and evil. Prayer is especially powerful from children and the disabled, as it gives a weapon to those the world marks as weak. In reality, we are all weak and in need of prayer.

We should only expect insults from the world when we take prayer seriously. Their unwillingness to address the issue of abortion directly is a reminder of the unreasonableness of their position. That they mock our prayer is a reminder of its effectiveness. We need not respond with anger nor let our peace be disturbed. Instead we should let it inspire us to cram more prayer into every corner of our day.

~ ~ ~

Daily Scripture:

And while being reviled, He did not revile in return; while suffering, He uttered no threats, but kept entrusting Himself to Him who judges righteously.

– *1 Peter 2:23*

Daily Intention:

Let me expect to be mocked, so I can overcome any fear of standing up to the culture of death.

Day 12

Fasting for Food Addicts

~ ~ ~

Fasting is powerful, especially against the demonic. Jesus tells us that some demons can only be driven out through prayer *and* fasting. The assault on human life, family, and human identity are demonic, so we *must* fast.

That's the good news.

The bad news is it seems impossible to actually do it. Few of us want to admit that fasting is difficult because it makes us look like the lame, lazy, and spoiled creatures we are.

Food is good, and I love it dearly. If you're an American, breathing, and not homeless, you probably have some sort of food addiction. (Remember that denial is the first stage.)

I have several food addictions. Meat, grease, salt, bread—unfortunately all are music to my ears. In fact, I enjoy talking about fasting because it means, first, we get to talk about food.

Food has a lot of power over us, and today we have the best of it available almost whenever and wherever we want. Because it is so hard to give it up, we need to be honest about how necessary fasting is in our current culture. It is not necessary because we need to diet or to lose weight or to be physically healthier. Rather, it is necessary to deny ourselves on behalf of a culture that is denying God of His due love and denying children of their lives.

I get tons of questions on fasting and write extensively about it in *The Beginning of the End of Abortion*. I don't tell people what to give up; of course, it is personal and some have health restrictions. But we shouldn't let fasting get lost as a discipline by offering up getting stuck in traffic or getting up earlier or not wearing the warmest clothes when it is cold. All of those are great things to do, but I strongly encourage you to give up some kind of food as well. Christians and Jews through the centuries have encouraged fasting, and Scripture gives us countless examples of why it is needed and good for the soul. Something about hunger is a uniquely effective reminder to pray for an end to abortion.

We can choose to skip a meal or skip multiple meals in a row, or we can commit to smaller sacrifices such as not getting a refill on a drink. Mortifying our desire for food is powerful—take it from me who detests any self-denial when it comes to food. Let's pick out some delicious food to give up. The angels will carry us through, and the demons will hate it.

~ ~ ~

Daily Scripture:

"Whenever you fast, do not put on a gloomy face as the hypocrites do, for they neglect their appearance so that they will be noticed by men when they are fasting. Truly I say to you, they have their reward in full. But you, when you fast, anoint your head and wash your face so that your fasting will not be noticed by men, but by your Father who is in secret; and your Father who sees what is done in secret will reward you."

    – Matthew 6:16–18

Daily Intention:

Today I will fast from a food, or portion of food, on behalf of those children who were denied a seat at the table through abortion.

Day 13

Humble and Proud of It

~ ~ ~

Humility. Right when we say we have it, we lose it.

As the Irish saying goes, "I'm humble and proud of it." Humility can be quite confusing for people, in part because the core of it is so hidden. It is not performative or careless or weak. Lying on the floor when plenty of chairs are available is not humble. Going without showering or combing your hair is not humble. Having no opinion or taking no position on anything is not humble.

There are many practical applications and definitions of humility, but Rick Warren has defined it as simply as possible: "Humility is not thinking less of yourself; it is thinking of yourself less."[1]

Humility is essential to building a culture of life. Only the most condescending, elitist, and arrogant people could tell other people not to breed. Only pride could lead to us dehumanizing the weak, the disabled, and the unfit so that we can kill them.

Humility is the key to pointing out the joy of life and of children. Babies are humble by nature. They love unconditionally and are completely dependent upon us. No wonder having kids is humbling!

Augustine summed it up: "If you should ask me what are the ways of God, I would tell you that the first is humility, the second is humility, and the third is humility. Not that there are no other precepts to give, but if humility does not precede all that we do, our efforts are fruitless."

Let us allow humility to precede all that we do, for our world and our future need humble warriors. Jesus Christ is our example. Let us reflect upon part of the famous Christian prayer, the Litany of Humility:

> *O Jesus! Meek and humble of heart, Hear me.*
> *From the desire of being esteemed, Deliver me, Jesus.*
> *From the desire of being loved, ℟.*
> *From the desire of being extolled, ℟.*
> *From the desire of being honored, ℟.*
> *From the desire of being praised, ℟.*
> *From the desire of being preferred to others, ℟.*
> *From the desire of being consulted, ℟.*
> *From the desire of being approved, ℟.*
> *From the fear of being humiliated, ℟.*
> *From the fear of being despised, ℟.*
> *From the fear of suffering rebukes, ℟.*
> *From the fear of being calumniated, ℟.*
> *From the fear of being forgotten, ℟.*
> *From the fear of being ridiculed, ℟.*
> *From the fear of being wronged, ℟.*
> *From the fear of being suspected, ℟.*

*That others may be loved more than I, Jesus grant me
the grace to desire it.*

That others may be esteemed more than I, ℞.

*That, in the opinion of the world, others may increase,
and I may decrease, ℞.*

That others may be chosen, and I set aside, ℞.

That others may be praised and I unnoticed, ℞.

That others may be preferred to me in everything, ℞.

*That others may become holier than I, provided that I
may become as holy as I should, ℞.*

O Jesus grant me:

Knowledge and love of my nothingness,

the continuous memory of my sins,

awareness of my selfishness,

the abhorrence of all vanity,

the pure intention of serving God,

perfect submission to the Will of the Father,

a true spirit of compunction,

blind obedience to my superiors,

holy hatred of all envy and jealousy,

promptness in forgiving offenses,

prudence in keeping silent about others' matters,

peace and charity toward everyone,

an ardent desire for contempt and humiliations,

the yearning to be treated like Thee,

and the grace to accept it in a holy way.

Let us pray.

Lord Jesus Christ, though being God, Thou didst humble Thyself even unto death—and death on the Cross—in order to be a constant example for us to confound our pride and self-love. Grant us the grace to imitate Thine example, so that by humbling ourselves as befits our wretchedness here on earth, we may be exalted and enjoy Thee in heaven forever.

Amen. [2]

~ ~ ~

Daily Scripture:

Do nothing from selfishness or empty conceit, but with humility of mind regard one another as more important than yourselves.

– *Philippians 2:3*

Daily Intention:

I will recite the Litany of Humility on behalf of those who have been led to the slaughter.

Day 14

Just Say No

~ ~ ~

If you're reading this book, you're struggling. And struggling is a gift.

I don't mean struggling in the sense of going through a dark, emotionally trying time. I mean struggling to fight against our selfishness, our laziness—to strive to be and do better. We don't struggle if we do what we want; decisions come easily and with affirmation. As Saint Josemaria famously said, "A saint is one who struggles."

Our struggle to be on time, get kids fed, get our tires rotated, take a relative to the doctor, pass the faith on to our kids, pick up groceries, pray every morning, read, budget for relatives visiting next weekend, all are a struggle—an often overlooked and heroic struggle. We must preserve our struggle to put our prayer life, our daily obligations, and our vocations to God and family *first*.

There is, however, quite a powerful word that can protect us from the many distractions pulling us astray: *no*.

Unless you're selfish or lazy, you are probably struggling to say no more often. No is often a path to sanity and holiness. "The Lord is not in noise," said Jean-Baptiste Chataurd, who wrote the spiritual classic *The Soul of the Apostolate*. Overcommitting, saying yes to everything and financing away our future hours and days without thought or prayer is not pro-life. It is pro-chaos.

I am not speaking from an ivory tower here but as a recovering overcommitter. From my first entrance into the pro-life movement, I have had beautiful opportunities to help, serve, or lead many worthy activities to build a culture of life. I was leading a local pro-life group at twenty-two and then 40 Days for Life went national. I did pretty much anything asked of me to help the cause and saw the word *no* as a curse word or a weakness. I had to learn (and am still learning) that we can only do so much, and we must protect our prior and more important obligation to those whom God has most entrusted to us.

We live in a culture of death; we need to pray and work as never before. But that work does not mean we must be everything at every opportunity in order to do good. That is the definition of losing focus.

Do not be afraid to say no (even if it means cutting back your 40 Days for Life commitment; we need prayer warriors, not the overwhelmed). The world is not dependent on you or me, and other people can do jobs that we are obliged to decline. You are no good to living a culture of life if you have no life. Be prudent in commitments, and God will use you in ways you never would have imagined.

~ ~ ~

Daily Scripture:

"I, wisdom, dwell with prudence,
And I find knowledge and discretion."
— *Proverbs 8:12*

Daily Intention:

I will say no to some small or large opportunity and prioritize my current commitments.

The Gift of Work

~ ~ ~

From as early as I can remember, my parents taught me to work hard. As kids our work ran the gamut: laundry, yardwork, schoolwork, cleaning the house.

Because the value of work was instilled in me at a young age, I've never been accused of being lazy. I've had various jobs from middle school, high school, and college, including grocery bagger, lawn mower, janitor, caretaker of a quadriplegic, door-to-door salesman in New Jersey (thick-skin developer), pizza delivery boy, and golf cart cleaner.

Most of us have had, or will have, jobs we love and jobs we hate. I love my current job and would work all the time if I wasn't a husband and father, but I never planned for this to be my job. I wanted to be a priest, then corporate lawyer, and ended up in the pro-life movement. If this job had been my plan, it probably never would have occurred.

No matter the job, when we work—and work well— we are building a culture of life. It is a witness to the value of the family when you dig a ditch, balance a budget, restructure a staff, create a new product, fix a toilet, or show up on time to your job to provide for your family. But even if you don't have family, being a good employer or employee is pro-life because it is a testament to the value of life.

John Paul II wrote extensively about the value of work and referred often to the impact manual labor had on him while living under Communism. In his encyclical *Laborem Exercens*, he said, "Man ought to imitate God both in working and also in resting, since God himself wished to present his own creative activity under the form of work and rest."

Many working men and women who, if they could, would devote more time to ending abortion often don't realize they are already rebuilding the culture of life by the effectiveness and Christian witness they have at work. We might not love the specific task at hand, but our work can be a true labor of love by our gratitude for such tasks and our striving for excellence as we complete them. Work protects us against idleness and laziness, and the degree of care and love we put into it imbues it with meaning and quietly reveals to ourselves and to others Who it is we ultimately work for.

~ ~ ~

Daily Scripture:

Nor did we eat anyone's bread without paying for it, but with labor and hardship we kept working night and day so that we would not be a burden to any of you.

– 2 Thessalonians 3:8

Daily Intention:

I will pray for those children scheduled to be aborted today as I encounter joys and frustrations in my workday.

Virginity Is Not
a Curse Word

~ ~ ~

I didn't live through it, but I'm told that the sexual revolution enshrined the attitude toward sex that all of us are supposed to assume today. That is, in order to be comfortable with sex, we must talk about it and do it with no objective restrictions on ourselves or, heaven forbid, others.

The homosexual movement carried out the logic of the revolt and further cemented it in our culture by declaring that freedom and equality demand the universal affirmation that we can have sex with whomever we want. To disagree is to be a first-class bigot. I'm too young to remember a time when our culture was supposedly uptight about sex. However, I am young enough to see the toll a free-sex society has had on us. The effectiveness of its propaganda might be most evident in the way in which it is considered a hang-up to consider, or even speak of, virginity.

Why are many so down on virginity? What did virginity ever do to anyone, and what relationship was ever harmed by it?

Today it seems if you are a virgin, encourage virginity, or advocate for virginity as the solution to much of our sexual dysfunction, you might as well be claiming that the earth is flat.

Virginity is about striving for and living virtue. It is not a list of prohibitions. My wife and I were both virgins when we married. I don't say that as a self-righteous claim but as a practical one. At no time did virginity make me ill, confused, miserable, sad, angry, lonely, or disrespected. Compare that with the devastating impact of "sexual freedom." The pain, hurt, and very real consequences of treating virginity like an old-fashioned term is written all over the parking lots of abortion facilities around the world.

I have known many virgins and recommitted virgins. They all had one thing in common: a desire to have clarity in their search for a spouse, without the confusion and pain that sex can cause when outside the context of marriage.

Virginity requires virtue and self-restraint but has as its fruit great joy, freedom, strength, and respect; these are just what we desperately need to characterize every dating relationship. Let's not be afraid to talk about virginity, advocate for virginity, and restore its rightful place as an integral part of our pursuit of authentic love.

~ ~ ~

Daily Scripture:

Let no one look down on your youthfulness, but rather in speech, conduct, love, faith and purity, show yourself an example of those who believe.

— *1 Timothy 4:12*

Daily Intention:

Today I pray for the restoration of virginity and ask for purity of heart no matter what my stage of life may be.

Day 17

Only Liars Escape This

~ ~ ~

The self-help industry has done a disservice to many souls. They have sold us the mundane and insane notion that if you think you're happy, then you're happy. This, of course, assumes that we truly can be happy in this world.

Typically, if we realize we're doing what the self-helpers are saying and are still unhappy, we need not worry. There is another book, catch phrase, psychological trigger, or training we can purchase to self-improve our way into happiness.

In this is lost the beautiful and meaningful reality of suffering . . .

Not suffering to better ourselves for this world but suffering to unite ourselves with the suffering of Christ. To preach Christ crucified as Saint Paul does. To embrace suffering with eternity as our focus as we go through our day. Daily sufferings are inevitable, and only a liar claims escape from this reality. But we must look at our sufferings squarely and put them in their proper context: as a gift and an opportunity to grow closer to Him.

That suffering is a gift can be difficult to believe when we're stuck in traffic, tending to a sick child, paying for a new transmission, or crying with a friend who has lost a spouse to cancer. It's hard to maintain the fantasy of a world without suffering when we listen to a woman who has had an abortion share her heart or a former abortion doctor describe this barbaric surgery in detail. There is no psychological manifestation to process this without a concept of *evil*.

Enduring our small and large sufferings with the heart of Jesus keeps us focused and at peace. In his classic, *The Imitation of Christ*, Thomas à Kempis says, "If you were really eager to get to heaven, you would relish with joy the struggles and conflicts of this world, never daring even once to complain; knowing in your inmost heart that where Christ is, in the kingdom with His Father, is where you will remain safe and at rest after your tribulations in this world are at an end."

Not only do we know we suffer, but Christ *allows* us to suffer.

~ ~ ~

Daily Scripture:

And He was saying to them all, "If anyone wishes to come after Me, he must deny himself, and take up his cross daily and follow Me."

– *Luke 9:23*

Daily Intention:

As I face sufferings today, I will remember that eternity with my Father in Heaven is my home and the source of my lasting happiness.

Day 18

God's Will

~ ~ ~

Attributing things to "God's will" can elicit varied reactions, from obedience to skepticism.

A friend of mine was the son of a Baptist preacher, and whenever his dad found a parking space he said, "Praise God! It's God's will we park here!" It drove my friend crazy. "Does God really care where we park?" he stewed.

Even if I exclude my own discernment of God's will for my life, I am well acquainted with His will for my life according to other people. I frequently hear that God has told someone to tell me to do something they themselves are unwilling to do. Isn't that nice of Him to do that?

God's will is not a trite phrase or a mere concept or joke. God willed us into existence, He willed us to our faith in Him, and He wills us to be breathing right now. He also willed that we live in this time in history, a time that is witnessing the largest slaughter of innocent children *ever*.

It is His will that abortion end and His will that we help bring about that end. To what capacity we help in this effort is for us to discern. We must simply do what Father John Hardon said is one of the hardest tasks, "To will the will of God."

That He wills our very existence imbues our lives with meaning and purpose. John Henry Newman rightly saw that being His creation is both an affirmation of our intrinsic worth and a mandate to serve: "Whatever I am, I can never be thrown away. If I am in sickness, my sickness may serve [God], in perplexity, my perplexity may serve Him. If I am in sorrow, my sorrow may serve Him. He does nothing in vain. He knows what He is about. He may take away my friends. He may throw me among strangers. He may make me feel desolate, make my spirits sink, hide the future from me. Still, He knows what He is about."

~ ~ ~

Daily Scripture:

And He who searches the hearts knows what the mind of the Spirit is, because He intercedes for the saints according to the will of God.

    – Romans 8:27

Daily Intention:

I will pray to will the will of God for what my role is in ending abortion in my community and country.

Day 19

Read Your Fuel

~ ~ ~

Half of Americans think that abortion is OK. (That statistic is higher in many other countries.)

Half!

Intellectually, abortion is the easiest thing to oppose. We have science, reason, faith, psychology, and personal experience on our side. But all of that is useless unless we equip ourselves by really absorbing and knowing the many and varied arguments and evidence that compel an honest thinker to oppose abortion.

We need to read. The greatest injustice in the history of the world, the most unnatural act in the history of mankind, is sustained by lies. We need to fuel ourselves with truth.

One of the most popular 40 Days for Life podcast episodes was one with our book suggestions: "The Top 5 Pro-Life Books."

Here we go . . .

5: *Three Approaches to Abortion* by Peter Kreeft

I love Peter Kreeft. He is my favorite modern author. I interviewed him for both a TV show and the podcast. This book is excellent, and in it he gives the moral, legal, personal, and logical positions to answer any abortion argument you would encounter. It is short and to the point. I'll stop there because otherwise I'll write about Peter Kreeft the rest of this book.

4: *Architects of the Culture of Death*
by Donald DeMarco (PhD) and Benjamin Wiker (PhD)

Not the most uplifting title in the world, but this is the definitive map of how we got here. This book is a must-read for anyone entering a typical college with the insanity on many campuses, promoting villains as heroes and lies as truths. Of the five, this book is the most academic.

3: *Pro-Life Answers to Pro-Choice Arguments*
by Randy Alcorn

Randy is a great author who is also a Protestant pastor. He masterfully argues for abortion in every scenario possible then systematically refutes each of his arguments. It is well researched, easy to understand, and a great reference tool. The last chapter is very powerful as he gives his reasons for opposing contraception.

2: *Unplanned* by Abby Johnson

I had the joy of living through the beautiful conversion story of Abby Johnson, who was the director of the Planned Parenthood in the town where I lived and worked. You can give this book to *anyone*. The book provides an accurate account, as does the major motion picture, *Unplanned*. Watch the movie or read the book. I suggest you do both.

1: *The Hand of God* by Bernard N. Nathanson, MD

This was the first pro-life material I gave to Abby Johnson when she walked into my office in 2009. I always loved this book, but her response just days after getting out of the abortion industry convinced me that this book is number one. Dr. Nathanson was the atheist who founded National Association for the Repeal of Abortion Laws (NARAL), the largest abortion advocacy group in America, and testified with fake numbers about illegal abortions to garner support for legal ones. He died a pro-life Catholic and is the first of many abortion doctors to have undergone such a radical and deep conversion.

All of these will not only prepare your mind but inspire you to be a voice for the voiceless. Happy reading!

Disclaimer: In an attempt to *not* be a lame and hopeless self-promoter, my books *40 Days for Life* and *The Beginning of the End of Abortion* are *not* on this list. (I know; it is quite humble of me.) With that said, I obviously suggest those, otherwise I would not have written them.

~ ~ ~

Daily Scripture:

Always be ready to give an explanation to anyone who asks you for a reason for your hope.

— *1 Peter 3:15 NABRE*

Daily Intention:

I will order and read one of these books.

Cynicism Takes No Effort

~ ~ ~

Abortion will end.

It will end in the United States, and the world will follow.

Do you believe that?

There are three thousand abortions per day in the United States. Do you believe that will end? Are you confident the nearly eight hundred abortion facilities in America will close, hospitals will stop doing abortions, and the pro-choice nightmare of "forced-birth" (their new, comically absurd term) will come true?

Do you believe that will happen? I do.

I can argue facts and share stories that support my confidence. I do that in my book *The Beginning of the End of Abortion*. But none of that really matters. You have to believe it. I don't mean psych yourself into believing it but rather something much deeper. You must have faith.

We must fight the all-too-common temptation of just saying, "We know how the book ends; we win." We need to know that deeply and work that reality into our daily lives.

Father Francis Fernandez reminds us our confidence has as its source an unexpected virtue: "A life of faith leads to a healthy superiority complex, born of a deep personal *humility*. Faith results from the deep conviction that one's efficacy comes entirely from God, not from oneself. This confidence leads the Christian to confront the obstacles he may encounter in his soul or in his apostolate with a will to win, even though the fruits of his efforts may be late in coming. With faith we will be able to move mountains, to bring down barriers which appeared insurmountable."[3]

Cynicism takes no effort. Despair is easy. Our pride allows us to rest in mediocrity. As followers of Christ, we must have the humility to have a disposition of *victory*.

If ending abortion is up to us, I'll give you one thousand reasons it will never end. But that would neglect the greatest event in history—the resurrection of Jesus Christ. That is the difference and the source of our confidence.

Our success is not from ourselves; when we embrace this truth, our prayers and small actions to end abortion will be multiplied. And when abortion ends, there will be but one reasonable explanation: God.

~ ~ ~

Daily Scripture:

Now faith is the assurance of things hoped for, the conviction of things not seen. For by it the men of old gained approval.

— *Hebrews 11:1–2*

Daily Intention:

I will share with one person today that I believe abortion will end. No matter the reaction, I will ask him or her to pray for it to occur.

Day 21

Highly Underrated Fun

~ ~ ~

When was the last time you went on a date?

Whether it be with a spouse, girlfriend or boy-friend, daughter or son, nephew or grandmother, how long has it been since you had a date?

On Valentine's Day the *Washington Post* highlighted research showing that young people are dating 56 percent less than previous generations in part because of social media and smartphones.[4] How depressing is that? We're not even dating anymore; we're just texting and living virtually and vicariously via pictures and videos on our phones. Had aliens been monitoring us over the years, they might be bewildered by how boring we have become.

The decrease in real human interaction, and just plain fun, represented by this decline in dating is dangerous for the future of the family.

We can do something about it, something that is a pleasure to do: go on a date! Go to a movie, a base-ball game, a bowling alley, an expensive steakhouse, a dumpy taco stand, or cook for your loved one and light candles. But do something before the computers take over!

We have so little time, and that makes dating all the more special and fun. I interviewed Father Paul Scalia, son of the late Justice Antonin Scalia, on the 40 Days for Life podcast. We asked him, "With abortion going on and children dying every day, can we go to a dinner with our wives? Can we sit back and relax with friends?" His answer was simple, "Yes." He expounded on that answer, but the point is we must live our lives to build a culture of life.

A culture where dating is on the decline and abortions are on the rise is a dying culture. We have forgotten how to court, impress, romance, and all the little awkward, fumbling nuances that go along with real human relationships. When we cook, put on music, and dance with our daughters in the kitchen, it is pro-life. When we go on a date or make our beloved a candlelit dinner, it is pro-life. A culture of life in general depends on flourishing relationships in particular.

So, surprise someone with flowers, a bottle of wine, dinner out, cooking in, candlelight, or a picnic. It is easy to dismiss these things as unnecessary, but the impact is lasting and needed to build a culture of life.

~ ~ ~

Daily Scripture:

Then he said to them, "Go, eat of the fat, drink of the sweet, and send portions to him who has nothing prepared; for this day is holy to our Lord. Do not be grieved, for the joy of the LORD is your strength."
  – *Nehemiah 8:10*

Daily Intention:

I will arrange a date to surprise someone I love.

Don't You Know
What Causes That?

~ ~ ~

Being parents of eight children, Marilisa and I have heard every funny, rude, and sarcastic comment out there from people we know and, awkwardly, from people we do not. It is rude to call a stranger fat but somehow OK to tell a stranger they have too many kids. We get "don't you know what causes that?," "you need a TV in your bedroom," "did you want all of those kids?," or "you're not going to have anymore, are you?" To which my sweet wife always responds, "We love our kids, and we are open to more if that's God's plan." My response is not as disciplined. I tend to say some version of, "I hope not! We don't even like our current kids. In fact, will you help us and take a few? Please, we're dying over here! We have boys and girls; just take your pick. Please! Please!" They always laugh or run off; either response is fine by me.

God created each of us and gave us the beautiful gift of being able to participate with Him in creation.

Of course, having one kid or ten kids is exhausting and a sacrifice. It also leaves us, quite beautifully, with a new vulnerability and purpose. Mother Teresa famously said, "Saying there are too many children is like saying there are too many flowers."

I'm not saying everyone needs to have one hundred kids; I know many couples who are struggling to have one. But a culture of life requires an openness to children. One trend today considers having children to be an act of irresponsibility. This mentality is backward. A culture without children or opposed to children is irresponsible. Life without them might be a seemingly safer or easier road, but it also is a road without the particular joy, pain, sacrifice, and love that they bring to a home. It is life lived with the fullness of love that makes a house become a home. A culture that rejects children is a culture that is homeless.

~ ~ ~

Daily Scripture:

Let the children come to me; do not prevent them, for the kingdom of God belongs to such as these.
– *Mark 10:14 NABRE*

Daily Intention:

I will thank my parents, grandparents, or friends who have kids for their sacrifice.

Day 23

Sundays and the Fourteenth Century

"Sunday was a day of rest;
now it's just one more day for progress."
— Rascal Flatts, "Mayberry"

~ ~ ~

It's true—Sunday has gotten lost. But because we are busier than ever before, we need rest more than ever before.

One struggle as Christians in the twenty-first century is living out and reminding our overworked, over-anxious, activity-driven world that Sunday is God's day and a day of rest. Keeping holy the Sabbath is essential for our families, our souls, and our sanity.

William Wilberforce dedicated his life to ending the injustice of slavery. He did so knowing the integral connection between fighting for a great cause and keeping the Sabbath. He stated so much by declaring, "O what a blessing is Sunday, interposed between the waves of worldly business like the divine path of the Israelites through the sea! There is nothing in which I would advise you to be more strictly conscientious than in keeping the Sabbath day holy. I can truly declare that to me the Sabbath has been invaluable."

Sundays are for church, prayer, family, food, and recreation. In the early years when 40 Days for Life was growing, I traveled on Sundays. It didn't take long to realize that was not pro-life. My kids at home and my wife taking them to Mass alone? Insane. Sunday must be protected.

God is not boring; He invented rest and rested Himself. There is not a more pro-life day than Sunday. When it starts to slip away as just another day for getting things done or getting a jump on the week, we need to reevaluate and reclaim our commitments to God and one another. I don't email on Sunday, I don't answer the phone on Sunday, and I try to live as though I am in the fourteenth century on Sunday.

There are circumstances when someone must work on a Sunday. But if we can at all avoid it, we should honor God and our families and live the fullness of life so that we might defend life more effectively. We are, in fact, commanded to do so. By living life in the fourteenth century for one day a week, we can be more engaged with the twenty-first century the rest of the week.

~ ~ ~

Daily Scripture:

Bring no burden from your homes on the sabbath. Do no work whatever, but keep holy the sabbath day, as I commanded your ancestors.

— *Jeremiah 17:22 NABRE*

Daily Intention:

I will go to church, cut out all work, and plan a good meal for this Sunday.

Day 24

Jesus, Remember Me

~ ~ ~

I know and am friends with several people who worked in and eventually left the abortion industry.

To date, 40 Days for Life has had the joy of helping two hundred abortion workers leave their jobs, the most well-known being Abby Johnson. Abby ran the Planned Parenthood where 40 Days for Life began. I knew her for eight years when she worked at Planned Parenthood before she walked into my office in 2009. She was the twenty-sixth person to leave the abortion industry during 40 Days for Life.

I have been asked hundreds of times, "How can they work there knowing what goes on? How can they look at the facts, the baby body parts, the reality of abortion and go to work as though this were some regular doctor's office?"

My answer is insufficient, but it is my answer: I don't know.

I don't know, and I don't pretend to know. I can give the typical explanation of falling into sin, having good intentions, wanting to help women. But for most people, even those who support abortion, participating in one and seeing a baby on the table afterward would send them sprinting to the nearest exit.

The road that leads into the abortion industry is one paved with pain. The devil is the architect of this road. No one grows up wanting to work in the abortion industry, and no doctor grows up wanting to be the best abortion doctor in the history of medicine. The exodus out of the abortion industry is huge, and the conversion gate only swings in one direction. I break down the "Movement of Converts" in *The Beginning of the End of Abortion.*

It's a natural question to ask how some people (starting with ourselves and our own sins) get to the place where they do what they do. I have heard many abortion workers explain and justify their jobs. I saw Abby Johnson swipe her security card for years going in and out of her abortion facility, a now-closed abortion facility that stands today as the headquarters for 40 Days for Life.

The important question we should carry daily is not why are they there, but *how do they get out?* The answer sits atop Calvary. The devil hates life, but even more than death of the body, he wants death of the soul. Sin led to Good Friday and Mercy was the result.

If we are to live a culture of life, we must pray and offer help for the babies scheduled to be aborted, the women and men seeking abortion, and the abortion workers. This is only possible with a merciful heart. Otherwise, we will be paralyzed by anger.

When you hear an abortion doctor interviewed or see a worker go into an abortion facility as you're praying outside, remember that you might be looking at someone who will one day be celebrating alongside you when abortion ends. That reality is the power of the mercy of Christ.

~ ~ ~

Daily Scripture:

"And indeed, we have been condemned justly, for the sentence we received corresponds to our crimes, but this man has done nothing criminal." Then he said, "Jesus, remember me when you come into your kingdom." He replied to him, "Amen, I say to you, today you will be with me in Paradise."

– *Luke 23:41–43 NABRE*

Daily Intention:

I will pray for God's mercy on my soul for my own sins. I will pray for all abortion workers who will participate today in this evil work. Help me remember that their work has no hope, but with Jesus's sacrifice on Calvary, their souls do.

Day 25

"Don't Worry about It"

~ ~ ~

When you're worried, this is the last phrase you want to hear. Usually, too, someone who has nothing at stake in the issue is the one telling you, "Don't worry about it."

We all worry about many serious and silly things.

I have met thousands of dedicated people who selflessly work to end abortion. They attend a march, participate in 40 Days for Life, adopt a child, or volunteer at a pregnancy resource center. But I have met even more pro-life people who have never done any such things. Why the lack of action?

For most of them I believe it is the overwhelming nature of the abortion issue. It is too heavy, and they think if they join the cause, it will crush their spirit and lead to despair.

Many of these people reached out to let me know how inspired they were after they read *The Beginning of the End of Abortion*. They couldn't believe the true stories and real progress being made in the pro-life cause. It helped them break out of the hopeless thinking and worry that a cliff is inevitable and looming where Jesus abandons us once and for all. It is simply not so.

We are approaching no cliff, and Jesus promises quite the opposite: "In My Father's house are many dwelling places; if it were not so, I would have told you."

"I would have told you"—a small sentence warning us away from our worries. If there was no hope, I would have told you. If your prayers were fruitless, I would have told you. There is indeed hope that the culture of life will prevail. So, don't worry about it, get busy, and trust His words when anxiety creeps in.

Trusting God and handing our concerns over to Him helps not only ourselves but also spreads out to our families, friends, parents, coworkers. Acting in faith and trust in God can bear fruit in surprising ways and places. Sometimes we might not see the fruit, but because we know Him, we can be confident that He is perfectly trustworthy and rest in that knowledge.

~ ~ ~

Daily Scripture:

In My Father's house are many dwelling places; if it were not so, I would have told you; for I go to prepare a place for you.

— *John 14:2*

Daily Intention:

I will not worry about the fruit of my prayers and efforts to end abortion. I will hand it to God and trust the words of Christ that, indeed, many rooms are in His Father's house. If I believe in that and live it today and every day, I can be confident we will be there together.

Day 26

Hope, Healing, and You

~ ~ ~

You know someone who has had an abortion.

You might not know who it is, but unless you are a hermit, you know at least one person, and have likely encountered dozens throughout your life, who have had abortions.

As a young man in college, I had the advantage of hearing five women share their testimonies about abortion. Despite being a college male already heavily active in the pro-life movement, these testimonies hit me hard.

Hearing a woman who has lain on that table share her experience and her pain will motivate you to help stop the next one before it occurs. That was my response then, and it still is today as I hear testimonials almost weekly.

When I speak at a dinner, visit a 40 Days for Life vigil, or participate in some event at my church, inevitably a woman pulls me aside to share her abortion experience. It always breaks my heart and sharpens my focus in this great cause. I have heard hundreds of testimonials from women (and men) and have tremendous respect for their honesty and courage in joining the fight against abortion. One of my favorite statistics at 40 Days for Life is that during every campaign for years at least 25 percent of our local campaign leaders were women who had an abortion.

I believe it is important for us who have not been directly impacted by abortion to hear these stories and know that there is likely no worse experience for a woman than undergoing an abortion.

Abortion is the poisonous fruit of loneliness and desperation. No one grows up wanting to violently end the life of her baby.

The healing process is a long and difficult cross to bear. When in conversation with people who disagree with us on abortion, we must remember that, very likely, an abortion experience is there and we need to treat them with love, respect, and mercy. I'm not saying that you assume everyone who supports abortion has had one. But sadly it is quite often the case, especially with those who are quick to become angry.

Jesus was meek and humble of heart. Let us never neglect the reality that we can be the first step to hope and healing for a person wounded by abortion.

~ ~ ~

Daily Scripture:

"To give his people knowledge of salvation
    through the forgiveness of their sins,
because of the tender mercy of our God
    by which the daybreak from on high will visit us
to shine on those who sit in darkness and death's
        shadow,
    to guide our feet into the path of peace."
    – *Luke 1:77–79 NABRE*

Daily Intention:

I am a disciple and must share the truth in love. Let me have the wisdom and mercy to respond with the heart of Christ to women (and men) who know the tremendous pain of abortion.

Big and Bad

~ ~ ~

Planned Parenthood.

Cecile Richards was one of the longest tenured CEOs for Planned Parenthood. She represented the corporate abortion mind-set no better than when she shared her own abortion experience: "I had an abortion. It was the right decision for me and my husband, and it wasn't a difficult decision."[5]

She then brushed off the decades of ongoing abortion debate with one word: *stigma*.

Abortion is defended in many ways, but it was the first time a corporate abortion leader has publicly described it as "not a difficult decision." Cecile should have visited some of her abortion facilities and told the women in the lobby and recovery room that their decision was not difficult. I'm sure it would have put them at ease. What woman who has participated in an abortion can relate to this? Such cold detachment and disconnect should give us hope.

As goes Planned Parenthood, so goes the abortion industry in America and around the world. In the United States, they operate 590 locations. Here are some staggering numbers from their own 2017–18 report:

- 332,757 abortions
- $1.67 billion in total income and tax funding ($563.8 million in taxes)
- Abortions made up 96 percent of pregnancy "resolution" services
- 1 adoption referral for every 117 abortions[6]

Planned Parenthood is abortion. That's why if a facility doesn't produce, they close. It is not about a cause; it is not about helping women or empowering anyone. It is about the money. If revenue drops, they do not stay open for the cause. They close.

In fact, they are doing so in record numbers. Since 1995, 37 percent of their locations have closed.[7]

I don't think anything hurts them more than showing up and praying outside. The movie *Unplanned* included something a former Planned Parenthood Employee of the Year, Abby Johnson, has been saying for years: When you pray outside of a Planned Parenthood, the "no-show" rate for an abortion appointment can go as high as 75 percent. A 75-percent no-show rate for just a small act of love!

This statistic reveals what God can do with our littleness when we trust Him and give a small portion of our time and attention to witness to His love in the darkest corners of our culture. A peaceful prayer presence has proven to be another way to defund Planned Parenthood. But more importantly, it has offered hope to those who show up for an abortion in despair. As many have testified, at that point it is not abortion but life that becomes the easy decision.

~ ~ ~

Daily Scripture:

Then it happened when the Philistine rose and came and drew near to meet David, that David ran quickly toward the battle line to meet the Philistine. And David put his hand into his bag and took from it a stone and slung it and struck the Philistine on his forehead. And the stone sank into his forehead, so that he fell on his face to the ground.

– *1 Samuel 17:48–49*

Daily Intention:

I will go and pray at my local abortion facility and trust God with the littleness of my effort. If I am unable, I will lift in prayer those who are standing outside and lovingly offering hope. I will pray for their victory in God's time.

Patriotism and Schizophrenia

~ ~ ~

Pro-life work is done first and foremost for love of God, but it is also done for love of country.

Supporting abortion is the worst thing you can wish upon any nation. Defending life is the most basic security any nation has.

Without children we have no future. The first and most fundamental right is the right to life. All other laws and rights *assume* life. We must work to create the best laws with regard to taxes, national security, health-care, criminal justice. These are important, but none of them are as important as the right to life. Without life we don't need tax reform, national security, better hospitals, or stronger law enforcement. Without life there is nothing to protect, respect, or cherish. All other issues work to enhance life. Because of this intrinsic incompatibility, when abortion comes into a nation, it makes that country schizophrenic.

Many countries will do everything possible to save a baby born prematurely. In some countries, including the United States, the miracle of modern medicine performs surgery on babies in the womb. Think about that. The baby has no rights according to the abortion industry, but if we *want* the baby to have a better life, she can get top notch medical care and even have surgery to enhance her life.

The best (or I should say worst) example of our schizophrenia I have seen was when I visited the 40 Days for Life campaign in Sacramento in 2010. On one floor was the neonatal clinic. A few floors down was a late-term abortion facility. You could see visibly pregnant women going into the building but could not tell if they were entering in an effort to get care and protection for their babies or if they were going in to have a late-term abortion. The babies on one floor got the best care our nation had to offer; the babies on the other floor were discarded as medical waste. Abortion makes a country schizophrenic.

Our fortitude and love of country can overcome this schizophrenia.

We speak out and fight against our laws not because we hate our country, but because we love it. Without a voice for the most voiceless citizens in our country, we have no future and no hope.

~ ~ ~

Daily Scripture:

They brought one to him and he said to them, "Whose image and inscription is this?" They replied to him, "Caesar's." So Jesus said to them, "Repay to Caesar what belongs to Caesar and to God what belongs to God." They were utterly amazed at him.

    – Mark 12:16–17 NABRE

Daily Intention:

I pray for the courage to be a voice for the voiceless in my nation in every election and in my role as a citizen. I will do this not for myself but for love of God and of my country.

Day 29

Abortion Is Hell

~ ~ ~

When the writers, directors, and producers of the film *Unplanned*, Cary Solomon and Chuck Konzelman, interviewed me for the movie, they concluded by saying they wanted to make a separate trip to visit the 40 Days for Life headquarters. They wanted to go inside the now-closed Planned Parenthood where 40 Days for Life began and where Abby Johnson was the director.

As they took pictures and footage (so they could rebuild the set for the movie), we got to the surgical room where most of the abortions were performed.

I explained where the table was and how they hung a baby mobile above the table for women to look at as the abortion was taking place. Cary said quietly but firmly, "This is Auschwitz." I told him that for me the saddest room was the next one.

In the recovery room, multiple sections all were divided by a curtain. In each section was a chair. There, after her abortion, each woman sat alone, yet among others, and "recovered." They were together in this room that curtains divided. They were together yet never more alone in their lives. Imagine the sounds—crying, texting, silence, breathing. Standing looking down at the floor, Cary said, "This is Hell."

I agree.

If you've seen *Unplanned*, you know how well Chuck and Cary recreated this Hell that is an abortion facility.

Hell, in our times, is usually only referenced in two trivial, nonthreatening ways, each a means of deflection. The first is when people casually joke about deserving it or looking forward to it, saying something like, "Hell will be great; all my friends will be there." The other is when it's referenced as just a way of describing something the speaker finds groan-worthy, such as study, work, or a dreaded weekend barbecue.

Most in our culture avoid overall serious consideration of Hell, but we know from the Gospels it is real. Jesus references Hell twenty times.[8] To paraphrase C. S. Lewis, the greatest trick of the devil is convincing us that Hell does not exist.

But Hell is real. That it is real only adds to, and makes necessary, the suffering, death, and resurrection of Christ. He died to save us—*all* of us. Abortion is from Hell, and despair, the essence of Hell, is what fuels abortion in this world. Despair in this life can be healed; despair in Hell is eternal. The late Jesuit Anthony Paone wrote, "The worst pain of Hell is not the torments. The people in Hell would gladly bear all of this if they could only hope for the friendship and love of Christ. Their keenest torment is that they have forever lost Christ, the Source of all true joy and perfect happiness. This suffering makes Hell the home of despair and hatred."[9]

When you pray for an end to abortion, when you perform a small act of love to end abortion, when you physically go out to pray at an abortion facility, be it for ten minutes or an hour, you declare war on the hopelessness of abortion and Hell.

Hope is what drives us because hope ends with Christ in Heaven. Hope is the fuel for our zeal for souls as we work to end abortion.

~ ~ ~

Daily Scripture:

Do not fear those who kill the body but are unable to kill the soul; but rather fear Him who is able to destroy both soul and body in hell.

– *Matthew 10:28*

Daily Intention:

I will pray for the wisdom and discipline to never forget the true source of abortion: Hell. Nor will I give into the temptation of despair when witnessing to the hope of life in a culture of death.

The Elephant in the Room

~ ~ ~

Melinda Gates, wife of Microsoft founder and billionaire Bill Gates, helped start one of the largest pro-life groups in Africa. All she did was give one interview. In her interview she not only advocated for but also offered to fund an effort to help spread artificial contraception throughout the continent of Africa.

Watching this interview was a young medical professional named Obianuju Ekeocha. Uju, for short, had her fire lit listening to this notion that the West was looking down on her people so much that they wanted to "help" by encouraging them not to breed. Uju went on to become the president of Culture of Life Africa.

Most people see contraception as a good thing or associate it with being educated or as something that helps a culture of life because it "prevents" abortion. In fact, many studies, including from Planned Parenthood's research arm, the Guttmacher Institute, show that more than half of the women who have abortions are already on contraception of some form.[10]

All Christian churches were unified against contraception until 1930. Now the widespread use of it is even prevalent among members of the Catholic Church, the last remaining Christian denomination to officially oppose contraception.

Because it is so common, most of us do not bother to question it, but we need to rethink artificial contraception. We are the only species that will use unnatural methods to avoid reproducing, the ultimate form of contraception being abortion.

There are physical risks to using artificial contraception with varying degrees of detriment to a woman's health. As awareness grows, so does the number of contraceptive-free couples who are nonreligious but simply seeking a more natural, organic lifestyle. It is also a fact that some forms of artificial contraception can cause an early abortion by preventing not ovulation or conception but the implantation of an already fertilized egg into the mother's uterus.[11]

While the physical ramifications are important reasons to be wary of contraception, they are not the most important. The physical harm of artificial contraception also is a reflection of a deeper reality pointing us to one thing: *Being open to God includes being open to children.*

Taking Him up on this great gift of co-creation eliminates as an option any artificial means to prevent such a gift. In a profound and beautiful way, being open to life makes us children too—we must be vulnerable, trusting, and more docile to His will. It is the ultimate and most rewarding way in which we trust our lives, marriages, and futures to Him.

Children are truly a blessing. That is not only a phrase on Hallmark cards; it is a biblical reality. We must dare to ask why, as an overall culture, we do *not* want kids.

We have a consensus that God should be Lord of our finances, Lord of our homes, Lord of our businesses, but what about Him being Lord of our fertility? There is a deep sadness in limiting that or cutting it off.

God entrusts us with children, but they are His. He can decide what that looks like for us.

Separating rampant use of artificial contraception from pro-life issues is naive at best and irresponsible at worst. A contraceptive mentality creates an abortive mentality by separating the act of sex from the possibility of children through actively blocking their existence. If children are a blessing, then that extends beyond whether they can be killed; it also compels us to examine how it is that we are or are not open to receiving them in our lives.

~ ~ ~

Daily Scripture:

Behold, children are a gift of the LORD,
The fruit of the womb is a reward.
Like arrows in the hand of a warrior,
So are the children of one's youth.
How blessed is the man whose quiver is full of them;

They will not be ashamed
When they speak with their enemies in the gate.
— *Psalm 127:3–5*

Daily Intention:

I will rethink artificial contraception, ask others to rethink it, or research the arguments against it.

Rape and Abortion

~ ~ ~

For most people, rape is the most difficult and uncomfortable aspect of the abortion issue to debate. It is also often one of the first things brought up in a conversation with an abortion supporter.

Despite the fact that rape cases make up about 1 percent of all abortions in a given year, the issue of rape is often used to justify all abortions. I've had hundreds of these conversations.

The statistics give an important context for understanding on one level; however, the seriousness with which we are called to discuss rape cannot be dismissed because the number is small. I have encountered many women who have been raped and the victims of sexual assault, and it is a deeply wounding and traumatic experience. Some chose to abort and others chose life. Here are some steps to keep in mind in such discussions.

Step 1: Affirm the crime and the situation

This is a different situation, a harder situation, because the woman is a living victim. We need to acknowledge that in conversation, in our tone as well as our words, and affirm that the man is the guilty party and should be in the penitentiary. He is the criminal and she is innocent. *She did nothing wrong.* I've learned that this is important to say because sometimes the person asking is a victim of rape and they sometimes blame themselves. Clearly pointing out the guilty party helps their healing and is a crucial part of the pro-life answer.

Step 2: Correct the myth that abortion removes a rape

I have encountered many testimonials, in person and online, from women who were raped, had an abortion, and came to deeply regret that decision. Violence against an innocent person cannot be remedied by using violence against another innocent person.

Step 3: Equality and dignity

We do not gradually gain dignity or value during gestation. We simply grow. Nor do we lose human dignity because of the circumstances of our conception. Our worth is not based on the crimes of our fathers except in the mind of the abortion industry, which claims that if you are a product of rape, your life is not worth protecting. We on the pro-life side, however, must witness to the truth that all unborn children are equal. A baby cannot have her dignity stripped from her because of the evil her father did.

Once we know how to effectively discuss this difficult topic, all other pro-abortion arguments become easy to counter. I've made these points with thousands of people, including in an interview on *NBC News*. The interviewer was not on our side, but she said she had never heard this perspective before. Trust that people don't know the truth, and when we share the truth with love, minds can be illuminated and hearts can be changed.

~ ~ ~

Daily Scripture:

Your kindness should be known to all. The Lord is near.

— Philippians 4:5 NABRE

Daily Intention:

I will pray for all who are victims of rape and sexual assault. I will defend their dignity as mothers, and the dignity of their unborn children, no matter the circumstances of conception.

Monday–Friday

~ ~ ~

Did you hear about the bus that crashed? First the bad news: Everyone on board was killed. The good news? It was a bus full of attorneys. Everyone cracks on lawyers until . . . they need one.

Two professions that have done much good and much evil are law and medicine. In my early years as a pro-life leader, I realized after a few legal threats from Planned Parenthood that our movement needed good pastors and good lawyers. Fortunately, we have both, but we need more.

Doctors and lawyers have always had an important role in society. Because of their importance, such paths usually include money, prestige, and a good deal of education.

However, the true need for doctors and lawyers today is not merely that we have them in larger numbers, but that we have more of them with a moral formation. Many have used law and medicine to attack the very institutions upon which society is built. To destroy a society, few ways are more effective than by attacking the fruits of marriage, but that is exactly what we have been doing by dehumanizing the child and redefining what marriage essentially is. If we can destroy the fruit, it is only a matter of time until we destroy the tree.

As G. K. Chesterton wisely said, "Take away the supernatural, and what remains is the unnatural."[12]

That medicine and law have corrupted much does not give us reason to run from them. Fleeing in that way would forfeit much and give in to a battle that must be fought and won on multiple levels, including within these two important fields. Much good can come from having good men and women who bring their moral formation into their professional fields. We all must live our faith every day, but we especially need doctors and lawyers to stand for God, life, and marriage not just on Sundays but also Monday through Friday.

Many "solid" Christians are in these two fields, but we need more. We need good lawyers who understand that law must be rooted in eternal truths. We need good doctors who take seriously their oath to "do no harm" and understand that the body in the womb is an integral part of a created person who has an Creator.

~ ~ ~

Daily Scripture:

After he had finished speaking, he said to Simon, "Put out into deep water and lower your nets for a catch." Simon said in reply, "Master, we have worked hard all

night and have caught nothing, but at your command I
will lower the nets."

— Luke 5:4–5 NABRE

Daily Intention:

I will pray for and thank any medical professionals or
lawyers who are witnessing to life in their careers. I will
look for opportunities to encourage someone consider-
ing a profession in medicine or law.

Day 33

Our Hand Doesn't Shake

~ ~ ~

The culture of death survives on anxiety, isolation, and despair.

Abortion facilities are physically designed for this. They have gates, escorts waiting at the door, and endless distractions once inside, even during the moment of the actual abortion. (I mentioned the baby mobiles hanging from the ceiling over the surgical table in another chapter.)

Anxiety runs wild in our culture, especially when it comes to abortion, in part because the effort required to distract us from truth is so great. Former abortion workers often feel an instant peace upon resigning. Many have told me that there always seemed to be a peace outside at our vigils—a peace never found inside the abortion facility.

The abortion industry wants us to believe the opposite. Abortion should provide relief. A problem is "solved" with a fifteen-minute surgery that removes our worries and secures our future as we want it.

But of course, peace comes from love and trust in God in *all* things.

Saint Josemaria Escriva says, "God has a right to ask us: Are you thinking about me? Are you aware of me? Do you look to me as your support? Do you seek me as the Light of your life, as your shield, as your all? Renew, then, this resolution: In times the world calls good I will cry out: 'Lord!' In times it calls bad, again I will cry: 'Lord'!"[13]

Without carrying our Lord with us, knowing He walks ahead of us, our many and varied lists of tasks and responsibilities can be overwhelming. Going it alone is inevitably anxiety producing. The only way we can fulfill our duties and have joy in our culture is by knowing we are doing His will and we are not doing it alone.

Seeing people live their lives and perform their duties with joy and peace is a powerful witness to His love. The more mundane the task, the more powerful the witness is for our anxious culture.

The devil attacks many of us with arrows of isolation and anxiety. We are not alone, however, because we walk with our Father in everything; our hand need not shake when we confront the tribulations of our times. Our personal trust in Him will make ripples today beyond what the eye can see.

~ ~ ~

Daily Scripture:

A violent squall came up and waves were breaking over the boat, so that it was already filling up. Jesus was in the stern, asleep on a cushion. They woke him and said to him, "Teacher, do you not care that we are perishing?" He woke up, rebuked the wind, and said to the sea, "Quiet! Be still!" The wind ceased and there was great calm. Then he asked them, "Why are you terrified? Do you not yet have faith?" They were filled with great awe and said to one another, "Who then is this whom even wind and sea obey?"

    – Mark 4:37–41 NABRE

Daily Intention:

I will carry my Lord with me today with life-affirming trust. When I am tempted to worry or get anxious about the minor or major things of my day, I will hand it over to Him who is always a few steps ahead of me.

A Good Start
to Saving Mankind

~ ~ ~

I get asked for reading lists all the time. Here's one to save the world.

This is *not* a list of the greatest books or of the greatest spiritual works of all time. Neither the Bible nor spiritual classics such as *The Imitation of Christ* are on here. Still, these books can wake us from our slumber in the modern world.

5: *Lost in the Cosmos* by Walker Percy
(recommended for college age and up)

If C. S. Lewis was a Catholic doctor from the South who had no filter, then his name would be Walker Percy. Get ready to laugh, cry, and perhaps be offended, all while thinking about bourbon and oysters. Percy lived and rests in Covington, Louisiana, and his writing reflects his Cajun madness . . . and genius. An excerpt:

"QUESTION: Who is the most obnoxious, Protestants, Catholics, or Jews?

ANSWER: As obnoxious as are all three, none is more murderous than the autonomous self who, believing in nothing, can fall prey to ideology and kill millions of people—unwanted people, old people, sick people, useless people, unborn people, enemies of the state—and do so reasonably, without passion, even decently, certainly without the least obnoxiousness."

4: *Orthodoxy* by G. K. Chesterton

A pagan turned agnostic turned Catholic, Chesterton wrote almost one hundred books and thousands of essays, none of which are dull. At only thirty-four years of age, he wrote *Orthodoxy* with his characteristic intellect and wit, putting Christianity up against everything the world has to offer.

In college I had a day-long discussion on the sidewalk with a Planned Parenthood volunteer who was an English professor. He gave me a book on atheism and told me to read the whole book. I did.

The next week I gave him *Orthodoxy* and told him to read only chapter 2, "The Maniac." Between escorting women in for abortions, he sat on the doorsteps of that Planned Parenthood abortion facility and read. Afterward he simply said, "I've never heard of Chesterton. I'm speechless."

3: *Brave New World* by Aldous Huxley

Despite having been disregarded by many academics when it was released in 1932, Huxley's classic is now seen as a work of prophetic genius. This satire gives alarming insight into who we are capable of marginalizing in order to live as we wish. An excerpt:

> "O brave new world," he repeated. "O brave new world that has such people in it. Let's start at once."
>
> "You have a most peculiar way of talking sometimes," said Bernard, staring at the young man in perplexed astonishment. "And, anyhow, hadn't you better wait till you actually see the new world?"

2: *The Abolition of Man* by C. S. Lewis

The greatest Christian writer of the twentieth century makes a compelling and effective attempt to save mankind in this classic. He shows what will occur if Western civilization ignores natural law and replaces it with each individual's will. To say he is prophetic is an understatement. An excerpt:

> "When all that says 'it is good' has been debunked, what says 'I want' remains. The Conditioners, therefore, must come to be motivated simply by their own pleasure. My point is that those who stand outside all

judgements of value cannot have any ground
for preferring one of their own impulses to
another except the emotional strength of
that impulse. I am very doubtful whether
history shows us one example of a man who,
having stepped outside traditional morality
and attained power, has used that power
benevolently."

1: *The Everlasting Man* by G. K. Chesterton

This is the book that is widely known for having
been the final straw for C. S. Lewis's conversion to
Christianity. *The Everlasting Man* is brilliant and some-
what forgotten. For anyone in the culture war, it gives
perspective to who and what we are fighting for. An
excerpt:

"I have said that Asia and the ancient world
had an air of being too old to die. Christendom has had the opposite fate. Christendom
has had a series of revolutions and in each
one of them Christianity has died. Christianity has died many times and risen again; for
it had a God who knew the way out of the
grave."

~ ~ ~

Daily Scripture:

But at daybreak on the first day of the week they took the spices they had prepared and went to the tomb. They found the stone rolled away from the tomb; but when they entered, they did not find the body of the Lord Jesus.

    – Luke 1:1–3 NABRE

Daily Intention:

I will order and read one of these books.

Day 35

Spiritual Warfare

~ ~ ~

The devil was arrogant enough to tempt Jesus.

He tempted Him in the desert, in the agony in the garden, and through the Pharisees who were constantly trying to trap and humiliate Christ. In following Him, we know that temptations come with the territory. Spiritual warfare is part of our citizenship in this world.

Our temptations, whether they be big or small, occur every day. We should never be too busy or too numb to recognize we are at war. However, we need to know who it is we are up against, and it is not those who hate us or disagree with us or who are actively working to destroy life.

We live in a label-happy society. By labeling someone—a bigot, sexist, racist, chauvinist, liberal, deplorable, homophobe, or anything else—we risk putting that person in a category and make the person the enemy rather than who we know the real enemy to be. Our focus in this fight should always be on the ultimate force of opposition: the devil.

This does not mean that we call our tipsy uncle a tool of the devil as he defends abortion at Thanksgiving. Nor does it mean we should be discouraged or paralyzed by fear, seeing temptations around every corner of our day. It does mean we keep in perspective who the true enemy of this world is but with the confidence that Christ's grace is always victorious.

Every morning when we wake up, we are tempted to worry about something, to feel behind, or to dread a task or even a person. Whether at work, with our kids, at the doctor, or stuck in traffic, we will be tempted to have our peace disturbed during the day. In his practical guide *The Spiritual Combat*, Lorenzo Scupoli writes, "The Lord will build up within your soul a city of peace, and your heart shall be a house of pleasures and delights. This He asks of you: that, when you feel agitated, you should begin again to quiet and calm yourself in all your actions and thoughts."[14]

The calm that comes from God is evident in the battle for life. This gentleness of spirit that comes from facing and overcoming temptation, or repenting when we give in to temptation, is powerful in our families. But it is also powerful when praying at an abortion facility or when defending life in our daily lives.

Agitation crushes calmness in our noisy world. Our willingness to know who our real enemy is and to trust God in moments of temptation will keep us focused on Christ, who defeated that enemy on Calvary.

~ ~ ~

Daily Scripture:

For our struggle is not with flesh and blood but with the principalities, with the powers, with the world rulers of this present darkness, with the evil spirits in the heavens.

– *Ephesians 6:12 NABRE*

Daily Intention:

Knowing the Lord walks ahead of me, I will call upon His name in the small or large temptations I face today. I will be confident He will not allow a temptation that I cannot overcome with His grace.

Day 36

A Daily Christmas

~ ~ ~

Every Christmas most of us take part in defeating the culture of death with two specific and indispensable Christmas activities. I don't mean seeing Santa Claus or listening to Bing Crosby, nor am I referring here to going to church.

I am talking about

1. praying together as a family in a home, and

2. eating a meal together as a family in a home.

Though these are basic and essential Christmas activities, we often neglect the importance of doing them together throughout the year. But compelling evidence shows time and again the truly transformative effects of such a simple thing as consistent family dinners. Research and studies show eating together as a family leads to

- better academic performance,

- lower risk of substance abuse,

- lower risk of teen pregnancy,
- lower risk of depression,
- high self-esteem for children.[15]

In a recent Columbia University study, 71 percent of teenagers said what they value most in a family dinner is talking, catching up, and spending time together.[16]

Rather than the exception reserved for a special occasion, eating dinner together should be our norm—one that we miss when travel or activities prohibit it from occurring. Dinner can be a daily oasis refreshing us with moments of levity and renewing our resolve for the next day by reminding us of the deeper and higher purposes to which we are committed.

If we work to save the world from every injustice out there and, in so doing, miss dinner every night at home, we are useless to the culture war. It is an important big-picture question to ask ourselves regularly, "How often do we all sit down together and have a meal?"

This takes sacrifice. It is no small feat. Meals don't just appear and then disappear. Good conversation is not without effort. We have to buy the food, cook the meal, set the table, clean the kitchen counters, sweep the dining room floor (ours can be comically messy after a meal), load the dishwasher, and unload it the next day. Plus, we have to be patient and kind and engaged with one another. Sometimes at the end of a busy day a more convenient meal can sound awfully attractive.

Understandably, a nightly family dinner is impossible every single day; still, it must be prioritized. It is a small pebble that, with time and consistency, builds a family, a future, and a country. It will not be picture perfect; it will be messy and inconvenient at times. But on our deathbed, prioritizing family dinners will never be a thing we regret.

Most of us pray and eat together as a family every Christmas. Even if our disposition is closer to that of an Ebenezer Scrooge, we might be consoled that even Scrooge converted. We need not relegate this effort to sit and share a meal to only one or two nights a year. The more we carry this part of Christmas (even if less formally) into the rest of our year, the more we can spread the joy and gratitude that Christmas brings into our homes and culture.

~ ~ ~

Daily Scripture:

For a child is born to us, a son is given to us;
    upon his shoulder dominion rests.
They name him Wonder-Counselor, God-Hero,
    Father-Forever, Prince of Peace.
His dominion is vast
    and forever peaceful,
Upon David's throne, and over his kingdom,
    which he confirms and sustains.

By judgment and justice,
    both now and forever.
The zeal of the LORD of hosts will do this!
    – *Isaiah 9:5–6 NABRE*

Daily Intention:

I will help plan, prepare, and clean up a family dinner in my home.

The Silent Weapon

~ ~ ~

Michael Jordan smokes six cigars per day.[17]

During his basketball career, he became the world's greatest basketball player, winning six NBA championships and five league MVP awards,[18] all the while smoking a cigar in his car on the way to every home game.

In multiple interviews, Jordan discusses his love for cigars. Why did he smoke before every game? Wasn't this a risk to his health and athleticism?

Here's his answer: "We had to be to the stadium at 6 o'clock for home games, and traffic was so bad it would take us an hour and fifteen or an hour and thirty minutes to drive. So now I'm sitting in a car for almost an hour and a half, and I'm very tense. I'm worried about the traffic. So, I started smoking a cigar going to the games. It became a ritual for every home game."

Traffic can be especially challenging to our activity-driven world. To keep us constantly distracted, our modern tendency is to cope with periods of waiting with some other activity available: smartphones, social media, music, small talk, nonstop and often sensationalized news stories, or [fill in your silence killer here]. But all of these fillers can keep us from the thing we need the most: an interior life with God. We might not need a cigar in our tense daily moments, but we all need silence and solitude.

Blaise Pascal summed it up, "All of humanity's problems stem from man's inability to sit quietly in a room alone."[19] Without silence we have no chance of seeing, hearing, or talking to God.

Noise is a roadblock to God. Our culture's incessant activity and noise make our intentional fostering of silence and solitude more important than ever before. On this dire need, Joseph Cardinal Ratzinger says, "In an age when the influence of secularization is always more powerful and one senses a diffused need to encounter God, may the possibility to offer spaces of intense listening to His Word in silence and prayer always be available."[20]

Constant noise not only distracts us from seeing our culture clearly but hinders our own creativity and discernment. Without silence, we find ourselves making big decisions or having important conversations without any thought, prayer, or preparation. Rick Warren offers the correct diagnosis and solution: "Open your mind to God. If you're going to do this, you've got to be quiet before the Lord. Schedule times of silence, of solitude. For many of you, God can't give you a dream because you won't sit down and shut up! You just need to be quiet before him."[21]

Abortion survives on the internal chaos of souls and societies that have no time or space for God. We need the clarity that comes when we resist distraction and make room for silence. Prayer orders our souls and our interior lives and is our great weapon in fighting the chaos and injustice that are the fruits of a world deaf to the voice of God.

~ ~ ~

Daily Scripture:

Be still and know that I am God!
   – *Psalm 46:11 NABRE*

Daily Intention:

Today I will bring silence into my day where I otherwise would not have had it. In the car, at my work, or in my home, I will find opportunities to foster silence, so I might listen and hear God.

A Family Matter

~ ~ ~

It only occurs once every decade or so, but when it does, I pay attention. What is this rare sighting? It is a media interview with notorious late-term abortion doctor LeRoy Carhart.

In his most recent interview, the abortionist directly answered the reporter's naive questions about reproductive rights and did not dance around the reality of what it is he does. (I write extensively on Carhart in *The Beginning of the End of Abortion*.)

Here is part of the transcript of Dr. LeRoy Carhart's interview with BBC reporter Hilary Andersson on July 22, 2019:

> *Carhart:* To the fetus it makes no difference whether it's born or not born. The baby has no input in this, as far as I'm concerned.
>
> *Hilary Andersson:* But it's interesting that you use the word baby because a lot of abortionists won't use that. They'll use the term fetus

because they don't want to acknowledge that there's a life.

Carhart: I . . . I think that it is a baby and I tell our . . . I use it with the patients.

Hilary Andersson: And you don't have a problem with killing a baby?

Carhart: (Pause) I have no problem if it's in the mother's uterus.[22]

When you watch this interview online, the reporter is taken aback and unsettled by his answers. In this exchange he reveals the heart of the matter of abortion: Might makes right.

Might makes right, so the one who is defenseless has no input as far as abortion is concerned. Carhart has no problem killing the baby, no problem saying he is killing the baby, no problem claiming the right to kill the baby. He has the might and therefore the right.

This is a rare moment when an abortion doctor does not try to conceal what it is he does with euphemisms. He also does not feel he needs to attempt to justify his work by shifting the conversation away from the baby to how he is really just helping the mother. The only reference here for Carhart about the baby's parents is when he says he has no problem "killing the baby inside the mother's uterus."[23] Think about how fundamentally unnatural that statement is.

This baby, according to him—and to many who support abortion—is never and can never be *someone's child*.

There is no *treasure* in this child. He or she is never considered a member of a family but merely an independent entity, on his or her own, unaware of what is about to happen and powerless to stop it. That the child is weak, is her weakness. And the weak will be dominated because the mighty have the power. In this is Carhart's, and the abortion movement's, greatest blindness to the unborn child.

You and I are not helpless in this. We don't have to read Carhart's comments, get mad, and storm around the house the rest of the day. We can oppose this injustice (rest assured we have 40 Days for Life campaigns outside Carhart's facilities to offer hope and to pray for him). More than that, however, you and I can love the children in our lives. The devil hates love and, therefore, hates the family. Jesus came into the world through the womb, through a family, and He designed human beings to be born into families. Abortion is the ultimate attack on this design by alienating us from our first and most naturally bonding and loving relationship.

Carhart gives us a correct assessment, one which reveals that abortion is straight from Hell. Christianity was birthed from Heaven in a barn, in poverty, in the cold, among animals, but with the one foundation God chose to use: *a family, a Holy Family*.

We started this chapter with Carhart but will end it with a man whose hope in God and family endured Nazism and Communism:

"The gist of family prayer is family life itself;
joys and sorrows, hopes and disappointments,
births and birthday celebrations, the wedding
anniversary of the parents, departures, sepa-
rations, homecomings, important decisions,
the death of loved ones. These moments
mark God's loving intervention in the family's
history. They should also be seen as suitable
moments for thanksgiving, for petition, for
trusting abandonment of the family into the
hands of their common Father in heaven. The
dignity and responsibility of the Christian
family as the domestic church can be achieved
only with God's unceasing aid, which will
surely be granted if it is humbly and trustingly
petitioned in prayer." – Saint John Paul II.[24]

~ ~ ~

Daily Scripture:

Love never fails. If there are prophecies, they will
be brought to nothing; if tongues, they will cease;
if knowledge, it will be brought to nothing. For we
know partially and we prophesy partially, but when
the perfect comes, the partial will pass away. When I
was a child, I used to talk as a child, think as a child,
reason as a child; when I became a man, I put aside
childish things. At present we see indistinctly, as in
a mirror, but then face to face. At present I know

partially; then I shall know fully, as I am fully known. So faith, hope, love remain, these three; but the greatest of these is love.

 – 1 Corinthians 13:8–13 NABRE

Daily Intention:

I will pray with and for my family today.

Day 39

We Know
What We Must Do

~ ~ ~

A great philosopher and music artist out of the 1990s, MC Hammer once sang, "We got to pray just to make it today."

Saint Teresa of Avila has been revered by Christians for centuries, and she was a little more direct (as Spaniards usually are) than MC Hammer. She said, "If you do not practice prayer, you don't need any devil to throw you into Hell, you throw yourself in there of your own accord."[25] This is a great one to remember as we are setting our alarms every night and are tempted to cut morning prayer.

Saint Teresa also had a gentler statement: "Give Jesus fifteen minutes alone every morning and he will give you Heaven." Saint Paul tells us to persevere in prayer (see 1 Thessalonians 5:17). Jesus tells us to pray, and the door will be opened (see Matthew 7:7).

"I'll pray for you" is a powerful statement that often is said too casually and with a subtext of, "I will forget I talked to you today," "You are lost and hopeless," "This conversation is over, and I no longer have to listen to you." This makes prayer seem like a weak dismissal rather than what it is: a great act of love and a vigorous aid to us all.

The bottom line is that prayer is powerful and not optional. We know it, but still it can't be repeated enough for all of us. Most of the time we need a kick in the rear from Teresa of Avila. It is her version of "Just Do It," but unlike a marketing slogan, it has eternal consequences. We must pray for our kids, relatives, culture, pastors, and for God's will in our daily lives. If we want to be in relationship with God, we must spend time with Him. Failure is not an option; without prayer we die spiritually, so let's do what we know we must do. We won't regret it.

~ ~ ~

Daily Scripture:

And He came to the disciples and found them sleeping, and said to Peter, "So, you men could not keep watch with Me for one hour?"
  – *Matthew 26:40*

Daily Intention:

I will get up fifteen minutes earlier tomorrow morning for prayer or add extra time for prayer. I pray that my soul, my family, and our culture might all benefit from this small sacrifice.

Day 40

To the Heart of the Matter

~ ~ ~

Imagining Heaven, or perhaps describing it to an inquisitive child, is inevitably challenging. Its depiction in movies and stories tends to be cheesy at best. The white robes, harps, and clouds make Heaven seem less like a real destination and more like a silly movie set.

The best description is the one that emphasizes how we cannot imagine it: "What eye has not seen, and ear has not heard, and what has not entered the human heart, what God has prepared for those who love him" (1 Corinthians 2:9 NABRE).

Heaven is our home and Christ our path. Mother Teresa said, "Do small things with great love." In this forty-day journey, we have prayed, laughed, and wept. We have resolved to live a culture of life in ways both large and small and, most importantly, to do those things with great love.

Our lives can only be complete if we live in Christ in all that we do, if we are willing to struggle, and if we are content with taking Him seriously—and ourselves not so much. He makes all the difference. As C. S. Lewis said, He is either liar, lunatic, or Lord. Because we know who He is, we must live accordingly.

This life will inevitably end for each of us with the four last things: Death, Judgment, and Heaven or Hell. We must trust that Jesus goes ahead of us, lighting our way. We must trust Him with our daily routines, our families, our schedules, our disappointments, our abortion crises, our culture's assault on the family. We must trust Him when things seem dark either in our personal lives or in our world.

I started this book saying these are difficult times but not hopeless times. You are in this moment of history for a reason. Your witness to family and to life and most importantly to the life, death, and resurrection of Jesus Christ is more powerful today than any other day because today is within your power!

Many are afraid to live authentic Christian lives in their families or in the public square. Be not afraid. Be not afraid in matters large or small. We only get so many days and so many hours; we need not waste them on fear. Instead we can take our day, our duties, our lists of tasks, our culture of death, and we can do small things with great love. We can go all in. We can give everything to Christ, we can fail, and we can try again.

We can—*every day*—go to the heart of the matter. We can—*out of joy*—sell all we have, buy that field, and inherit the kingdom of Heaven.

~ ~ ~

Daily Scripture:

"The kingdom of heaven is like a treasure buried in a field, which a person finds and hides again, and out of joy goes and sells all that he has and buys that field."
— *Matthew 13:44*

Daily Intention:

I will pray part of the classic Christian Universal Prayer:

Lord, I believe in Thee: may I believe more strongly. I trust in Thee: may I hope more confidently. I love Thee: may I love Thee more ardently. I am sorry for my sins: May I have a deeper sorrow.

I adore Thee as my first beginning. I long for Thee as my last end. I praise Thee as my constant benefactor. I invoke Thee as my gracious protector.

Guide me by Thy wisdom, restrain me with Thy justice, comfort me with Thy mercy, protect me with Thy power.

I offer Thee, Lord, my thoughts, that they may rise to Thee; my words, that they may speak of Thee; my actions, that they may follow Thy Will; my sufferings, that they may be borne for Thee.

*I want to do what Thou will, because
Thou will it, in the way Thou will it,
for as long as Thou will it.*

*I beg of Thee, Lord, to enlighten my
understanding, to inflame my will, to
purify my heart, and to sanctify my soul.*

*I beg Thee that pride may not infect me;
that neither flattery may affect me, not the
world deceive me; and that the devil
may not trap me in his snares.*

*Grant me the grace to purify my memory,
to guard my tongue, to take custody of my
eyes, and to mortify me senses.*

*May I weep for my past sins, resist future
temptations, correct my evil inclinations,
and cultivate the virtues I should have.*

*O God, grant that I may love Thee and
despise myself, have love for my neighbor,
and contempt for the world.*

*May I strive to obey my superiors, assist
those under me, be attentive to my friends,
and forgiving of my enemies.*

*May I conquer sensuality with austerity,
greed with generosity, anger with meekness,
and tepidity with fervor.*

Make me prudent in my decisions,
steadfast in dangers, patient in adversity,
and humble in prosperity.

O Lord, make me attentive at prayer,
temperate at my meals, diligent in my
duties, and firm in my resolutions.

May my conscience be pure, my exterior
modest, my conversation edifying,
and my life well-ordered.

May I be ever-watchful in mastering
my natural impulses, corresponding to
Thy grace, keeping Thy law,
and obtaining salvation.

May I learn from Thee
the nothingness of this world,
the greatness of heaven,
the shortness of time,
and the length of eternity.

Through Christ our Lord.
Amen.[26]

Acknowledgments

~ ~ ~

I'm thankful to God and my parents for the gift of my life and the opportunity to serve this greatest cause of my generation.

Special thanks goes to so many in my travels who told me to write a book like this but could never explain to me quite what they meant. I ignored you for years then finally got what you were saying.

Writing this book came at one of the busiest times of my life (and I said that during the last book). 40 Days for Life had more campaigns around the world than ever before, and we had just launched a new magazine, app, online store, and podcast. Marilisa and I were also awaiting the delivery of our eighth baby. I could not have done this without the support of the 40 Days for Life headquarters team: Steve Karlen, Robert Colquhoun, Dr. Haywood Robinson, Sue Thayer, Melinda Giambo, Bobby Reynoso, Dawn Crawford, Lourdes Varela, Jill Copeland, Andrea Fisher, Gilbert Gonzales, Ben Starnes, and of course Cheryl the Great (Tamez) who has been with us since the very beginning. We have a great team, a team who truly struggles to live and practice what they preach.

To Matt Britton, Carol Siedhoff, Segundo de los Heros Monereo, Mark Spearman, and Alfonso Chicharro, who work hard to serve our leaders and have a deep desire to offer hope to women and their babies. I'm thankful for their many sacrifices.

To our donors who make the growth and improvement of 40 Days for Life possible. Our donors are not distant from our mission; they are participants, and we never forget that.

For the heroes of 40 Days for Life: the local campaign leaders. You inspired this project by how you live your life while leading campaigns.

Thank you to my editor Noelle Mering, a very prolife name and a soul who was perfect for this project. To Lisa Parnell, who copyedited and typeset the book. Thank you, Wes Yoder of Ambassador Agency. What a journey. I appreciate your email response when I gave you the quick idea for this book: "Love it!"

Thank you to my children. This book is dedicated to you. Please continue to pray, dance, laugh, and clean your rooms without being told. Mom and I love all of you very much and are blessed that God entrusted you to us.

In thanksgiving for the many holy priests in our life—your joy and faith are contagious. In thanksgiving for the centuries of saints who have gone before us and given us a road map to follow Christ every day.

Finally, thank you to Marilisa, my wife who still thinks I'm funny and has continued to date me since I first asked her out. I love you.

Endnotes

~ ~ ~

1. Rick Warren, *The Purpose Driven Life: What On Earth Am I Here For?* (Grand Rapids: Zondervan, 2009).

2. *Prayers* (Plymouth, MI: Miles Christi, 2013), 41–44.

3. Francis Fernandez, *In Conversation with God*, vol. 4 (London: Scepter Press, 1989), 343.

4. Arthur C. Brooks, "The U.S. is in a crisis of love," February 13, 2019, https://www.washingtonpost.com /opinions/the-us-is-in-a-crisis-of-love/2019/02/13/06b9 2e3e-2ef1-11e9-8ad3-9a5b113ecd3c_story.html?noredirect =on.

5. Cecile Richards, "Ending the Silence That Fuels Abortion Stigma," October 16, 2014, https://www.elle .com/culture/career-politics/a15060/cecile-richards -abortion-stigma/.

6. https://www.plannedparenthood.org/uploads/ filer_public/80/d7/80d7d7c7-977c-4036-9c61-b3801741 b441/190118-annualreport18-p01.pdf

7. Emily Ward, "Report: Planned Parenthood Operates Over Half of U.S. Abortion Clinics, February 15, 2019, https://www.cnsnews.com/news/article/emily

-ward/report-planned-parenthood-operates-over-half-us
-abortion-clinics.

8. Michael Allen Rogers, "What Did Jesus Teach about Hell?, May 27, 2014, https://www.crossway.org/articles/what-did-jesus-teach-about-hell/.

9. Anthony J. Paone, *My Daily Bread: A Summary of the Spiritual Life* (Brooklyn: Confraternity of the Precious Blood, 1954), 38–39.

10. Guttmacher Institute, "About Half of U.S. Abortion Patients Report Using Contraception in the Month They Became Pregnant," January 11, 2018, https://www.guttmacher.org/news-release/2018/about-half-us -abortion-patients-report-using-contraception-month-they -became.

11. Alexandra Desanctis, "Yes, Some Contraceptives Are Abortifacients," November 4, 2016, https://www.nationalreview.com/2016/11/contraception-birth-control -abortion-abortifacients-ella-plan-b-iud-embryo-life/.

12. G. K. Chesterton, *Heretics*, https://www.goodreads.com/quotes/911395-take-away-the-supernatural -and-what-remains-is-the-unnatural.

13. Josemaria Escriva, *The Forge* (Le Laurier Press), 506.

14. Lorenzo Scupoli, *Spiritual Combat: How to Win Your Spiritual Battles and Attain Inner Peace* (Manchester, NH: Sophia Institute Press, 2002), 183.

15. "Benefits of Family Dinners," https://thefamilydinnerproject.org/about-us/benefits-of-family-dinners/.

16. Mirele Mann, "9 Scientifically Proven Reasons to Eat Dinner as a Family," May 5, 2016, https://www.goodnet.org/articles/9-scientifically-proven-reasons-to-eat -dinner-as-family.

17. Marvin R. Shanken, "Michael Jordan: The Sequel," November/December 2017, https://www.cigar aficionado.com/article/michael-jordan-the-sequel.

18. Marvin R. Shanken, "One-on-One with Michael Jordan," July/August 2005, https://www.cigaraficionado .com/article/one-on-one-with-michael-jordan-6189.

19. https://www.goodreads.com/quotes/19682-all -of-humanity-s-problems-stem-from-man-s-inability-to-sit

20. https://zenit.org/articles/papal-address-to -spiritual-exercises-federation/

21. Lighthouse Trails editors, "Rick Warren Says He Practices Silence and Solitude," February 1, 2007, https://www.lighthousetrailsresearch.com/blog/?p=3383.

22. Hilary Andersson, Panorama, "America's Abortion War," July 22, 2019, https://www.bbc.co.uk/iplayer/ episode/m00071k9/panorama-americas-abortion-war?fbcli d=IwAR1OX5JybUY9H6LfFZ5rabtbEnJSlK2owZ0oDuEn NVCDqgNLw8M4U7N3lks.

23. Sarah Terzo, "Infamous abortionist stuns BBC reporter by admitting he 'kills babies,'" August 16, 2019, https://www.liveaction.org/news/abortionist-stuns-bbc -admitting-kills-babies/.

24. John Paul II, Apostolic Exhortation, *Familiaris Consortio* (November 22, 1981), 59.

25. Jean-Baptiste Chataurd, *The Soul of the Apostolate* (Charlotte, NC: Tan Books, 2012), 85.

26. *Prayers* (Plymouth, MI: Miles Christi, 2013), 37–40.

About the Author

~ ~ ~

Shawn Carney is the co-founder, CEO, and president of 40 Days for Life. He began as a volunteer in the pro-life movement while still in college. During this time he helped to lead the first-ever local 40 Days for Life campaign. After graduating from college, Shawn was asked to serve as the executive director of the Coalition for Life, a local pro-life organization in Texas made up of more than sixty churches.

In 2019, Shawn and his wife Marilisa were portrayed in the movie *Unplanned*, for their role in helping former Planned Parenthood director Abby Johnson during her conversion. Abby was the twenty-sixth out of more than two hundred abortion workers to date who have reached out to 40 Days for Life.

Shawn is a regular media spokesperson, and his work has been featured on hundreds of outlets including *NBC News*, *Fox News*, *Fox & Friends*, the *Glenn Beck Show*, the *Laura Ingraham Show*, BBC, the Drudge

Report, *The Guardian*, *USA Today*, and Christian media, including *The Christian Post*, *National Catholic Register*, Sirius XM Catholic Radio, EWTN Radio, and Focus on the Family.

Shawn is one of the most sought after pro-life speakers today, addressing audiences coast-to-coast and internationally. He has executive produced and hosted award-winning pro-life documentaries and is the host of the weekly 40 Days for Life podcast. Shawn is the co-author of *40 Days for Life: Discover What God Has Done . . . Imagine What He Can Do* and the author of the national best-seller *The Beginning of the End of Abortion*. He is a member of the Knights of Columbus and the Equestrian Order of the Holy Sepulchre of Jerusalem. Shawn lives in Texas with his wife and eight children.

40 DAYS FOR LIFE

Be part of the beginning of the end of abortion!

PRAY MORE!

Find your closest 40 Days for Life vigil today at
40daysforlife.com/locations

READ MORE!

Keep up with saved lives, abortion worker conversions, and the pulse of the pro-life movement by receiving *DAY 41*, the quarterly magazine, for FREE! Sign up at
40daysforlife.com/magazine

LISTEN MORE!

Download the weekly 40 Days for Life podcast for free. Guests include Peter Kreeft, Eric Metaxas, Alan Keyes, Father Paul Scalia, Benjamin Watson, Lila Rose, and many more. Listen on any podcast app, the 40 Days for Life app, or at
40daysforlife.com/podcast

Get special discounted copies of this book and the national best-seller *The Beginning of the End of Abortion* and great pro-life gear at
40daysforlifegear.com

Invite Shawn Carney or another member of the 40 Days for Life headquarters team to speak at your event by emailing
media@40daysforlife.com
Find out more at 40daysforlife.com

143